Addition and Subtraction Speed Drills to Build Fact Fluency

Kindergarten and 1st Grade Workbook

Age 5-7

Timed Tests

Mazes

Home Run Press™, 2020

Want Free Extra Goodies for Your Student?

Email us at: info@homerunpress.com.

Title the email "Addition and Subtraction Speed Drills to Build Fact Fluency"

and we'll send some extra worksheets your way!

We create our workbooks with love and great care.

For any issues with your workbook, such as printing errors, typos, faulty binding, or something else, please do not hesitate to contact us at: info@homerunpress.com.

We will make sure you get a replacement copy immediately.

THANK YOU!

First published in the USA 2020.   ISBN 9781952368110

Table of Contents

Understanding Addition and Subtraction. 10 + 1; 9 + 2; 8 + 3; 7 + 4; 6 + 5

Number Bonds. Mazes. CogAT test prep   6-17

Understanding Addition and Subtraction. 10 + 2; 11 + 1; 9 + 3; 8 + 4; 7 + 5; 6 + 6. Number Bonds. Mazes. CogAT test prep   18-26

Understanding Addition and Subtraction. 10 + 3; 11 + 2; 12 + 1; 9 + 4; 8 + 5; 7 + 6. Number Bonds. Mazes. CogAT test prep   27-35

Understanding Addition and Subtraction. 10 + 4; 11 + 3; 12 + 2; 11 + 3; 9 + 5; 8 + 6; 7 + 7. Number Bonds. Mazes. CogAT test prep   36-44

Understanding Addition and Subtraction. 10 + 5; 11 + 4; 12 + 3; 13 + 2; 14 + 1; 9 + 6; 8 + 7. Number Bonds. Mazes. CogAT test prep   45-53

Understanding Addition and Subtraction. 10 + 6; 11 + 5; 12 + 4; 13 + 3; 14 + 2; 15 + 1; 9 + 7; 8 + 8. Number Bonds. Mazes. CogAT test prep   54-62

Understanding Addition and Subtraction. 10 + 7; 11 + 6; 12 + 5; 13 + 4; 14 + 3; 15 + 2; 16 + 1; 9 + 8. Number Bonds. Mazes. CogAT test prep 63-70

Understanding Addition and Subtraction. 10 + 8; 11 + 6; 12 + 6; 13 + 5; 14 + 4; 15 + 3; 16 + 2; 15 + 1; 9 + 9. Number Bonds. Mazes. CogAT test prep   71-76

Understanding Addition and Subtraction. 10 + 9; 11 + 8; 12 + 7; 13 + 6; 14 + 5; 15 + 4; 16 + 3; 17 + 2; 18 + 1. Number Bonds. Mazes. CogAT test prep   77-80

Understanding Addition and Subtraction. 10 + 10; 11 + 9; 12 + 8; 13 + 7; 14 + 6; 15 + 5; 16 + 4; 17 + 3; 18 + 2; 19 + 1. Number Bonds. Mazes. CogAT test prep   81-91

Answers   92

Hi. I'm Sunny. For me, everything is an adventure. I am ready to try anything, take chances, see what happens - and help you try, too! I like to think I'm confident, caring and have an open mind. I will cheer for your success and encourage everyone! I'm ready to be a really good friend!

I've got a problem. Well, I've always got a problem. And I don't like it. It makes me cranky, and grumpy, impatient and the truth is, I got a bad attitude. There. I said it. I admit it. And the reason I feel this way? Math! I don't get it and it bums me out. Grrrr!

Not trying to brag, but I am the smartest Brainer that ever lived - and I'm a brilliant shade of blue. That's why they call me Smarty. I love to solve problems and I'm always happy to explain how things work - to help any Brainer out there! To me, work is fun, and math is a blast!

I scare easily. Like, even just a little …Boo! Oh wow, I've scared myself! Anyway, they call me Pickles because I turn a little green when I get panicky. Especially with new stuff. Eek! And big complicated problems. Really any problem. Eek! There, I did it again.

Hi! Name's Pepper. I have what you call a positive outlook. I just think being alive is exciting! And you know something? By being friendly, kind and maybe even wise, you can have a pretty awesome day every day on this amazing planet.

A famous movie star once said, "I want to be alone." Well, I do too! I'm best when I'm dreaming, thinking, and in my own world. And so, I resist! Yes, I resist anything new, and only do things my way or quit. The rest of the Brainers have math, but I'd rather have a headache and complain. Or pout.

1. <u>Write</u> the numbers from 0 to 10.

0 __ __ __ __ __ __ __ __ __ __

2. <u>Write</u> these numerals. <u>Trace</u> the number words.

zero   one   two   three   four   five

six   seven   eight   nine   ten

3. <u>Join</u> the numbers with a line. <u>Start</u> at 0 and <u>finish</u> at 10.

5   6   9   4

    1   0   10

2   8   3   7

1. <u>Trace</u>. <u>Write</u> in the missing numbers. <u>Color</u> the squares.

10 + 1 = 11   eleven   eleven

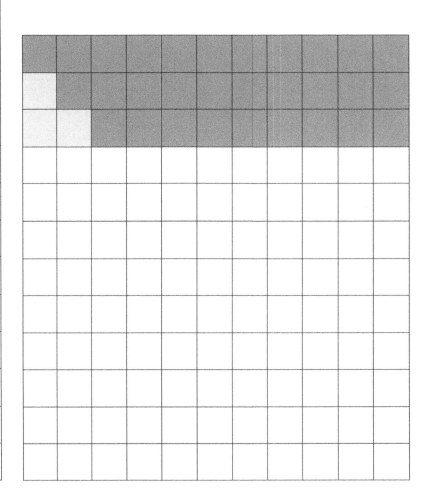

11
0
1
2
3
4
5
6
7
8
9
10
11

2. <u>Make and write</u> the smallest and the biggest two-digit numbers you can with any two of these digits: 0, 1, 5.

Answer: _____

First, make ten! I need to add two more to 8 to get 10.

So, I decompose a smaller number.

3 is 2+1

I take "2" out of the "3" and put "2" to the "8": 2 + 8

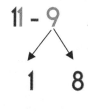

Now I have 10 and "1" leftover: 10 + 1 = 11

So, 3 + 8 is the same thing as 10 + 1.

Answer: 2 + 8 + 1 = 10 + 1 = 11

I need to subtract 9 ones out of 11 ones.

I decompose 9. 9 is 1 + 8.

First I take away 1 out of 11 to make 10. But to take away a total of 9, I have to take away 8 more.

11 – 1 - 8 = 10 – 8 = 2

1. <u>Write</u> the missing numbers.

$0 + 11 =$ __	$11 - 0 =$ __
$1 + 10 =$ __	$11 - 1 =$ __
$2 + 9 = 1+9+\_ =$ __ 1 1	$11 - 2 = 11-1-\_ =$ __ 1 1
$3 + 8 = 2+8+\_ =$ __ 2 _	$11 - 3 = 11-1-\_ =$ __ 1 _
$4 + 7 = 3+7+\_ =$ __ 3 _	$11 - 4 = 11-1-\_ =$ __ 1 _
$5 + 6 = 4+\_+\_ =$ __ 4 _	$11 - 5 = 11-\_-\_ =$ __ 1 _
$6 + 5 = 6+\_+\_ =$ __ 4 _	$11 - 6 = 11-\_-\_ =$ __ 1 _

www.homerunpress.com

1. <u>Write</u> the missing numbers.

$11 + 0 =$ ___ | $11 - 11 =$ ___

$10 + 1 =$ ___ | $11 - 10 =$ ___

$7 + 4 = 7 + \_ + \_ =$ ___ | $11 - 7 = 11 - \_ - \_ =$ ___
$\quad\quad\quad | \quad |$ | $\quad\quad\quad\quad\quad | \quad |$
$\quad\quad\quad 3 \quad \_$ | $\quad\quad\quad\quad\quad 1 \quad \_$

$8 + 3 = 8 + \_ + \_ =$ ___ | $11 - 8 = \_ - \_ - \_ =$ ___
$\quad\quad\quad | \quad |$ | $\quad\quad\quad\quad\quad | \quad |$
$\quad\quad\quad 2 \quad \_$ | $\quad\quad\quad\quad\quad 1 \quad \_$

$9 + 2 = \_ + \_ + \_ =$ ___ | $11 - 9 = \_ - \_ - \_ =$ ___
$\quad\quad\quad | \quad |$ | $\quad\quad\quad\quad\quad | \quad |$
$\quad\quad\quad 1 \quad \_$ | $\quad\quad\quad\quad\quad 1 \quad \_$

$6 + 5 = \_ + \_ + \_ =$ ___ | $11 - 7 = \_ - \_ - \_ =$ ___
$\quad\quad\quad | \quad |$ | $\quad\quad\quad\quad\quad | \quad |$
$\quad\quad\quad \_ \quad \_$ | $\quad\quad\quad\quad\quad \_ \quad \_$

$8 + 3 = \_ + \_ + \_ =$ ___ | $11 - 4 = \_ - \_ - \_ =$ ___
$\quad\quad\quad | \quad |$ | $\quad\quad\quad\quad\quad | \quad |$
$\quad\quad\quad \_ \quad \_$ | $\quad\quad\quad\quad\quad \_ \quad \_$

1. <u>Write</u> the missing numbers.

1 + 10 = __	11 - 1 = __
10 + 1 = __	11 - 10 = __
2 + 9 = _ + _ + _ = __	11 - 6 = _ - _ - _ = _
3 + 8 = _ + _ + _ = __	11 - 8 = _ - _ - _ = _
5 + 6 = _ + _ + _ = __	11 - 3 = _ - _ - _ = _
4 + 7 = _ + _ + _ = __	11 - 2 = _ - _ - _ = _
7 + 4 = _ + _ + _ = __	11 - 5 = _ - _ - _ = _

1. <u>Write</u> the missing numbers.

4 + 7 = __ + __ + __ = __   11 - 9 = __ - __ - __ = __

5 + 6 = __ + __ + __ = __   11 - 3 = __ - __ - __ = __

8 + 3 = __ + __ + __ = __   11 - 6 = __ - __ - __ = __

2 + 9 = __ + __ + __ = __   11 - 8 = __ - __ - __ = __

6 + 5 = __ + __ + __ = __   11 - 5 = __ - __ - __ = __

3 + 8 = __ + __ + __ = __   11 - 7 = __ - __ - __ = __

7 + 4 = __ + __ + __ = __   11 - 2 = __ - __ - __ = __

2. <u>Write</u> the missing numbers. The arrow means: __ is greater than __.

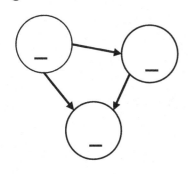

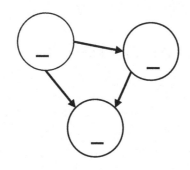

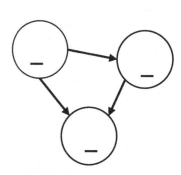

11, 9, 5   6, 11, 3   10, 8, 11

1) Write ones under ones.

2) Carry over when the sum is 10 or more.

3) Find out how many more you need to add to a greater number to get a ten.

```
     ones
      8
  +   3
  _____
  -
```

Step 1: I need one more row above 8 to write the numbers that were carried over.

Step 2: First, I add ones: 8+3=8+2+1=11. I created a whole new ten, and it will go in the tens column.

```
tens  ones
 -
       8
  +    3
  _____
 -     -
```

Write the 1 in one's place. Carry 1 ten with the tens. Write the 1 in the ten's column.

```
tens  ones
 1
       8
       3
  _____
 -     1
```

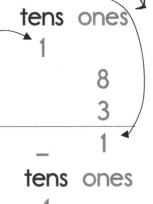

Step 3: Add up the tens column: 1+0+0=1.

```
tens  ones
 1
       8
  +    3
  _____
 1     1
```

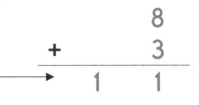

1. <u>Write</u> the missing numbers. __ plus what equals __?

9	5	4	8	7
+	+	+	+	+
1 1	1 1	1 1	1 1	1 1

8	1 0	2	7	8
+	+	+	+	+
1 1	1 1	1 1	1 1	1 1

4	9	8	6	5
+	+	+	+	+
1 1	1 1	1 1	1 1	1 1

2.

<u>Circle</u> the correct answer:

I have a series of numbers: 2, 5, 8, __

<u>What</u> is the next number?

A) 10   C) 9

B) 12   D) 11

1. <u>Write</u> the missing numbers. __ plus what equals __?

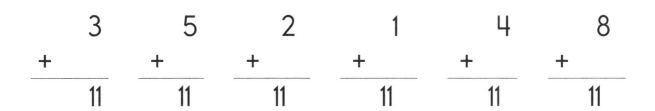

3	5	2	1	4	8
+	+	+	+	+	+
11	11	11	11	11	11

11	6	9	7	10	11
+	+	+	+	+	+
11	11	11	11	11	11

2. <u>Complete</u> each pair of number bonds.

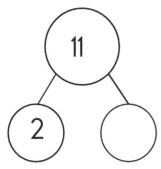

_ and 1 make 11

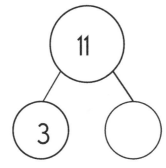

3 and __ make 11

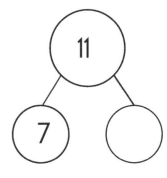

7 and __ make 11

2 and __ make 11

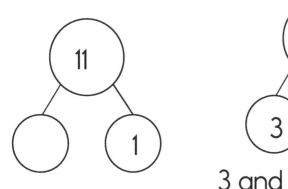

4 and __ make 11

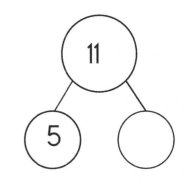

5 and __ make 11

1) Write the smaller number under the larger number;

2) Ones under ones, tens under tens;

3) Subtract ones, then tens.

tens	ones
1	1
-	9
--	--

In the columns we subtract 9 ones out of 1.

tens	ones
1̄	1̄
-	9
--	--

Step 1: If I subtract in columns, I need one more row above 11.

Step 2: Borrow/Take 1 ten out of the tens since 11=10+1.

Write 11 above 1 in one's place since 10 ones and 1 ones are 11.

tens	ones
	10+1
1	1
-	9
--	--

Step 3: leave 0 above 1 in ten's place. Cross out 1 and 1 to avoid mistakes.

Step 3: Subtract 9 ones from 11 ones:

11-9=2. Do NOT rewrite 0 in the ten's column.

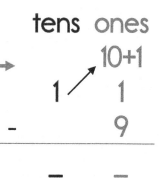

tens	ones
0	11
1̶	1̶
-	9
	2

1. <u>Subtract.</u>   Score ___/15   Time __:__

0 11	‾ ‾	‾ ‾	‾ ‾	‾ ‾
1̶ 1̶	1 1	1 1	1 1	1 1
- 8	- 5	- 9	- 2	- 7
3				

‾ ‾	‾ ‾	‾ ‾	‾ ‾	‾ ‾
1 1	1 1	1 1	1 1	1 1
- 6	- 3	- 4	- 8	- 5

‾ ‾	‾ ‾	‾ ‾	‾ ‾	‾ ‾
1 1	1 1	1 1	1 1	1 1
- 4	- 6	- 3	- 9	- 2

2.

Circle the correct answer:

I have a series of numbers:
1, 6, __.

<u>What</u> is the next number?

A)   10   C)   11
B)   12   D)   9

       www.homerunpress.com

1. Subtract.

11	11	11	11	11	11
- 7	- 5	- 3	- 1	- 2	- 4

11	11	11	11	11	11
- 0	- 6	- 8	- 10	- 9	- 11

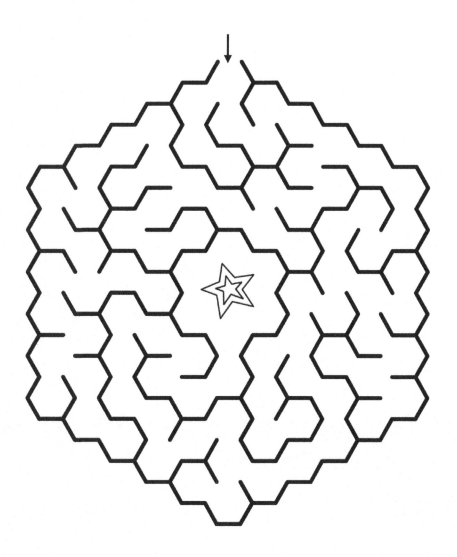

1. <u>Trace</u>. <u>Write</u> in the missing numbers. <u>Color</u> the squares.

10 + 2 = 12   twelve   twelve

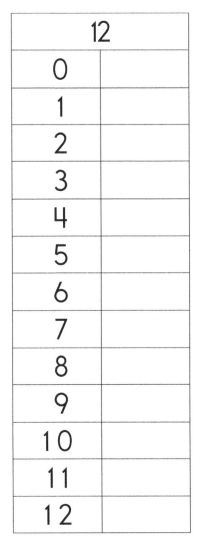

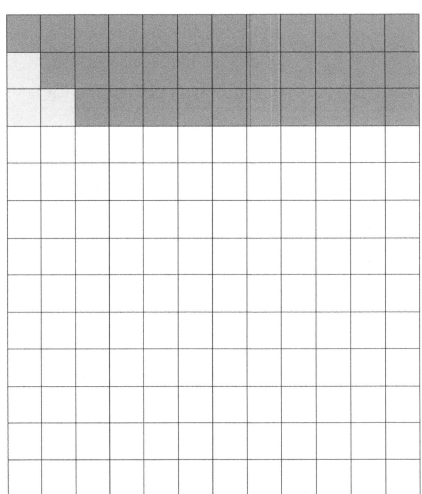

2. <u>What</u> is the value of the digit 2 in the numbers below? <u>Circle</u> your answer.

12   ones/tens   25   ones/tens

www.homerunpress.com

1. <u>Write</u> the missing numbers. <u>Add</u> or <u>subtract</u>.

10 + 2 = __	12 - 2 = __
11 + 1 = __	12 - 1 = __

$3 + 9 = 1 + 9 + 2 =$ __ | $12 - 3 = 12 - 2 - 1 =$ __
| | | | |
1   2   2   1

$4 + 8 = 2 + 8 + \_ =$ __ | $12 - 4 = 12 - 2 - \_ =$ __
2   _   2   _

$5 + 7 = 3 + \_ + \_ =$ __ | $12 - 5 = 12 - \_ - \_ =$ __
3   _   2   _

$6 + 6 = 4 + \_ + \_ =$ __ | $12 - 6 = 12 - \_ - \_ =$ __
4   _   2   _

$7 + 5 = 7 + \_ + \_ =$ __ | $12 - 7 = 12 - \_ - \_ =$ __
_   _   _   _

1. <u>Write</u> the missing numbers. <u>Add</u> or <u>subtract</u>.

12 + 0 = __	12 - 12 = __
0 + 12 = __	12 - 0 = __

8 + 4 = _ + _ + _ = __   12 - 8 = 12 -_ - _ = __

    2   _   2   _

9 + 3 = _ + _ + _ = __   12 - 9 = _ - _ - _ = __

    _   _   _   _

6 + 6 = _ + _ + _ = __   11 - 9 = _ - _ - _ = __

    _   _   _   _

8 + 4 = _ + _ + _ = __   12 - 8 = _ - _ - _ = __

    _   _   _   _

7 + 5 = _ + _ + _ = __   12 - 7 = _ - _ - _ = __

    _   _   _   _

    www.homerunpress.com

1. Write the missing numbers. Add or subtract.

1 + 11 = __   12 - 1 = __

10 + 2 = __   12 - 10 = __

3 + 9 = _+_+_ = __   12 - 6 = _-_-_ = _
  | | | |
_ _   _ _

5 + 7 = _+_+_ = __   12 - 8 = _-_-_ = _
  | | | |
_ _   _ _

4 + 8 = _+_+_ = __   12 - 3 = _-_-_ = _
  | | | |
_ _   _ _

3 + 9 = _+_+_ = __   11 - 5 = _-_-_ = _
  | | | |
_ _   _ _

6 + 6 = _+_+_ = __   11 - 7 = _-_-_ = _
  | | | |
_ _   _ _

1. <u>Write</u> the missing numbers. <u>Add</u> or <u>subtract</u>.

3 + 9 = __ + __ + __ = __   12 - 9 = __ - __ - __ = __

5 + 7 = __ + __ + __ = __   12 - 3 = __ - __ - __ = __

8 + 4 = __ + __ + __ = __   12 - 6 = __ - __ - __ = __

6 + 6 = __ + __ + __ = __   12 - 8 = __ - __ - __ = __

7 + 5 = __ + __ + __ = __   12 - 5 = __ - __ - __ = __

9 + 3 = __ + __ + __ = __   12 - 7 = __ - __ - __ = __

8 + 4 = __ + __ + __ = __   12 - 4 = __ - __ - __ = __

2. <u>Write</u> the missing numbers. The arrow means: __ is "greater than" __.

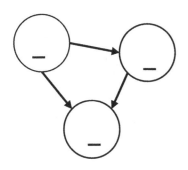
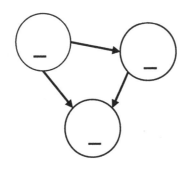
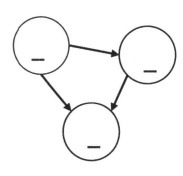

1, 4, 8   2, 7, 11   12, 10, 5

www.homerunpress.com

1. <u>Add.</u> <u>Write</u> the missing numbers.

```
    ‾            ‾            ‾            ‾            ‾
    3            6            4            5            9
+   9        +   5        +   8        +   7        +   2
_____        _____        _____        _____        _____


    ‾                         ‾            ‾            ‾
    8            2            2            5            6
+   3        + 1 0        +   9        +   6        +   6
_____        _____        _____        _____        _____


    ‾            ‾            ‾            ‾
    9            6            8            6          1 0
+   3        +   5        +   4        +   6        +   1
_____        _____        _____        _____        _____
```

2.

Circle the correct answer:

I have a series of numbers:

0, 6, __

<u>What</u> is the next number?

A)   10   C)   9
B)   12   D)   11

1. <u>Write</u> the missing numbers. __ plus what equals __?

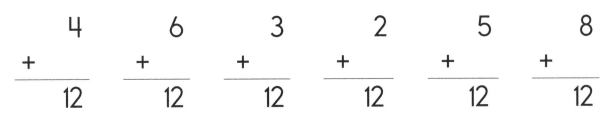

4	6	3	2	5	8
+	+	+	+	+	+
12	12	12	12	12	12

12	6	9	7	10	4
+	+	+	+	+	+
12	12	12	12	12	12

2. <u>Complete</u> each pair of number bonds.

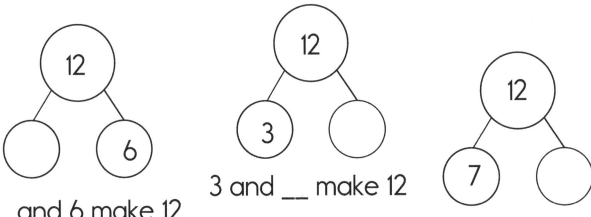

_ and 6 make 12

3 and __ make 12

7 and __ make 12

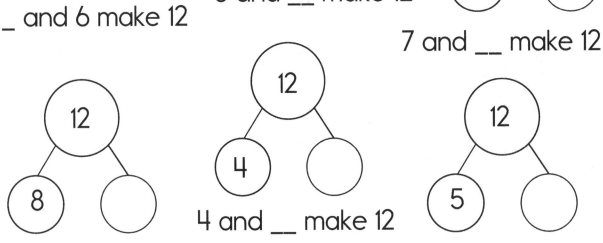

8 and __ make 12

4 and __ make 12

5 and __ make 12

www.homerunpress.com

1. <u>Subtract.</u>   Score ___/15   Time __:__

$$\begin{array}{r} \bar{1}\ \bar{2} \\ -\quad 8 \\ \hline \end{array} \qquad \begin{array}{r} \bar{1}\ \bar{2} \\ -\quad 5 \\ \hline \end{array} \qquad \begin{array}{r} \bar{1}\ \bar{2} \\ -\quad 9 \\ \hline \end{array} \qquad \begin{array}{r} \bar{1}\ \bar{2} \\ -\quad 2 \\ \hline \end{array} \qquad \begin{array}{r} \bar{1}\ \bar{2} \\ -\quad 7 \\ \hline \end{array}$$

$$\begin{array}{r} \bar{1}\ \bar{2} \\ -\quad 6 \\ \hline \end{array} \qquad \begin{array}{r} \bar{1}\ \bar{2} \\ -\quad 3 \\ \hline \end{array} \qquad \begin{array}{r} \bar{1}\ \bar{2} \\ -\quad 4 \\ \hline \end{array} \qquad \begin{array}{r} \bar{1}\ \bar{2} \\ -\quad 8 \\ \hline \end{array} \qquad \begin{array}{r} \bar{1}\ \bar{2} \\ -\quad 5 \\ \hline \end{array}$$

$$\begin{array}{r} \bar{1}\ \bar{2} \\ -\quad 4 \\ \hline \end{array} \qquad \begin{array}{r} \bar{1}\ \bar{2} \\ -\quad 7 \\ \hline \end{array} \qquad \begin{array}{r} \bar{1}\ \bar{2} \\ -\quad 3 \\ \hline \end{array} \qquad \begin{array}{r} \bar{1}\ \bar{2} \\ -\quad 9 \\ \hline \end{array} \qquad \begin{array}{r} \bar{1}\ \bar{2} \\ -\quad 6 \\ \hline \end{array}$$

2.

Circle the correct answer:

I have a series of numbers:
0, 2, 4, 7, __.

What is the next number?

A)   11   C)   10
B)   12   D)   9

1. <u>Subtract.</u>

12	12	12	12	12
- 7	- 5	- 3	- 8	- 6

12	12	12	12	12
- 4	- 9	- 3	- 5	- 7

www.homerunpress.com

1. <u>Trace</u>. <u>Write</u> in the missing numbers. <u>Color</u> the squares.

10 + 3 = 13   thirteen   thirteen

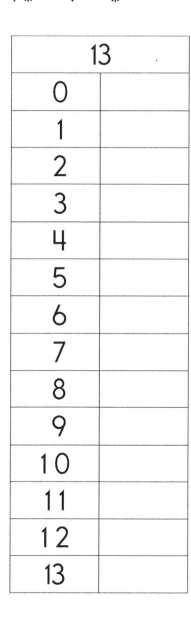

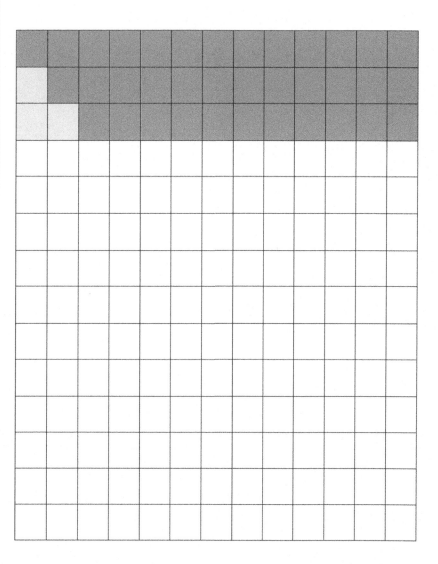

2. <u>Underline</u> all the combinations that equal 9.

4 + 5   5 + 6   6 + 3   2 + 7

1. <u>Write</u> the missing numbers. <u>Add</u> or <u>subtract</u>.

$10 + 3 =$ __	$13 - 10 =$ __
$12 + 1 =$ __	$13 - 12 =$ __

$4 + 9 = 1 + 9 + 3 =$ __ $13 - 4 = 13 - 3 - 1 =$ __
  | | | |
 1 3   3 1

$5 + 8 = 2 + 8 + $_$ =$ __ $13 - 5 = 13 - 3 - $_$ =$ __
 | | | |
 2 3   3 2

$6 + 7 = 3 + $_$ + $_$ =$ __ $13 - 6 = 13 - $_$ - $_$ =$ __
 | | | |
 3 _   3 _

$4 + 7 = $_$ + $_$ + $_$ =$ __ $13 - 7 = $_$ - $_$ - $_$ =$ __
 | | | |
 _ _   _ _

$8 + 5 = $_$ + $_$ + $_$ =$ __ $13 - 8 = $_$ - $_$ - $_$ =$ __
   | | | |
   _ _   _ _

     www.homerunpress.com

1. Write the missing numbers. Add or subtract.

11 + 2 = __	13 - 2 = __
0 + 13 = __	13 - 0 = __

9 + 4 = 9 + _ + _ = __
     | |
    1   _

13 - 9 = 13 - _ - _ = __
     | |
    3   _

8 + 5 = _ + _ + _ = __
     | |
    _   _

13 - 8 = _ - _ - _ = __
     | |
    _   _

7 + 6 = _ + _ + _ = __
     | |
    _   _

13 - 7 = _ - _ - _ = __
     | |
    _   _

5 + 7 = _ + _ + _ = __
  | |
 _   _

13 - 5 = _ - _ - _ = __
     | |
    _   _

4 + 9 = _ + _ + _ = __
  | |
 _   _

13 - 4 = _ - _ - _ = __
     | |
    _   _

1. <u>Write</u> the missing numbers. <u>Add</u> or <u>subtract</u>.

$3 + 10 = \underline{}$	$13 - 3 = \underline{}$
$1 + 11 = \underline{}$	$13 - 1 = \underline{}$
$7 + 6 = 7 + \_ + \_ = \underline{}$ $\quad\quad\quad 3 \quad \_$	$13 - 7 = 13 - \_ - \_ = \underline{}$ $\quad\quad\quad\quad 3 \quad \_$
$9 + 4 = \_ + \_ + \_ = \underline{}$ $\quad\quad\quad \_ \quad \_$	$13 - 6 = \_ - \_ - \_ = \underline{}$ $\quad\quad\quad\quad \_ \quad \_$
$8 + 5 = \_ + \_ + \_ = \underline{}$ $\quad\quad\quad \_ \quad \_$	$13 - 9 = \_ - \_ - \_ = \underline{}$ $\quad\quad\quad\quad \_ \quad \_$
$4 + 9 = \_ + \_ + \_ = \underline{}$ $\quad\quad \_ \quad \_$	$13 - 8 = \_ - \_ - \_ = \underline{}$ $\quad\quad\quad\quad \_ \quad \_$
$6 + 7 = \_ + \_ + \_ = \underline{}$ $\quad\quad \_ \quad \_$	$13 - 4 = \_ - \_ - \_ = \underline{}$ $\quad\quad\quad\quad \_ \quad \_$

www.homerunpress.com

1. Write the missing numbers. Add or subtract.

8 + 5 = __ + __ + __ = __   13 - 9 = __ - __ - __ = __

9 + 2 = __ + __ + __ = __   12 - 3 = __ - __ - __ = __

6 + 7 = __ + __ + __ = __   12 - 6 = __ - __ - __ = __

3 + 8 = __ + __ + __ = __   13 - 8 = __ - __ - __ = __

5 + 7 = __ + __ + __ = __   11 - 5 = __ - __ - __ = __

7 + 4 = __ + __ + __ = __   13 - 7 = __ - __ - __ = __

9 + 4 = __ + __ + __ = __   11 - 6 = __ - __ - __ = __

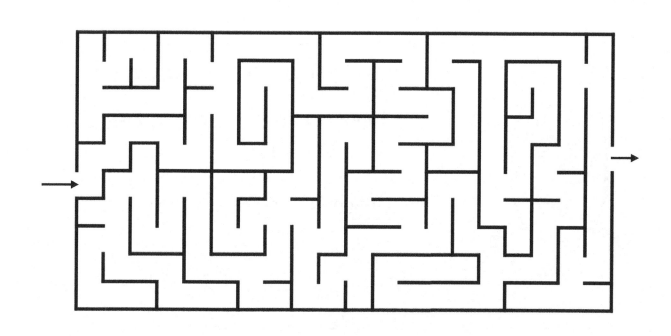

1. <u>Add.</u> <u>Write</u> the missing numbers.

```
    ¯            ¯            ¯            ¯            ¯
    3            6            5            4            8
+   9        +   7        +   6        +   7        +   4
_____      _____      _____      _____      _____


    ¯
    8            2            3            ¯            ¯
                                         6            4
+   5        + 1 0        + 1 0        +   5        +   9
_____      _____      _____      _____      _____


  1 0          ¯            ¯            ¯          1 2
               6            8            9
+   3        +   6        +   5        +   2        +   1
_____      _____      _____      _____      _____
```

2.

Circle the correct answer:

I have a series of numbers:
1, 4, 8, __

<u>What</u> is the next number?

A)   10   C)   13
B)   12   D)   11

www.homerunpress.com

1. <u>Add.</u>

```
    5          6          4          1          8          9
  + 8        + 6        + 9       + 10        + 5        + 3
  ___        ___        ___        ___        ___        ___
```

```
   10          7          8          8         11          0
  + 1        + 6        + 4        + 5        + 1       + 13
  ___        ___        ___        ___        ___        ___
```

2. <u>Complete</u> each pair of number bonds.

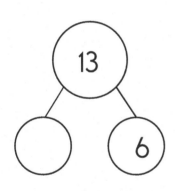

_ and 6 make 13

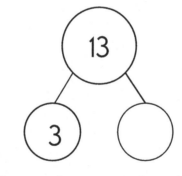

3 and __ make 13

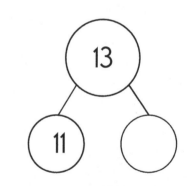

11 and __ make 13

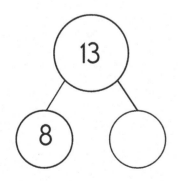

8 and __ make 13

4 and __ make 13

10 and __ make 13

1. Subtract.   Score ___/15   Time __:__

```
  0  13
  1̶  3̶        ‾  ‾        ‾  ‾          ‾  ‾
            1  3        1  3      1  3      1  3
-      8    -     5    -     9   -     2   -     7
─────────  ─────────  ────────  ────────  ────────
       5
```

```
  ‾  ‾                    ‾  ‾       ‾  ‾      ‾  ‾
  1  3      1  3        1  3       1  3      1  3
-      6    -     1    -     4    -     8   -     5
─────────  ─────────  ─────────  ────────  ────────
```

```
  ‾  ‾       ‾  ‾                  ‾  ‾       ‾  ‾
  1  3      1  3      1  3        1  3       1  3
-      4    -     7   -     3    -     9    -     6
─────────  ────────  ────────  ─────────  ─────────
```

2.

Circle the correct answer:

I have a series of numbers:
2, 3, 5, 8, __.

What is the next number?

A)   10   C)   11

B)   12   D)   9

       www.homerunpress.com

1. Subtract.

| 13 | 13 | 13 | 13 | 13 |
| - 7 | - 5 | - 3 | - 8 | - 6 |

| 13 | 13 | 13 | 13 | 13 |
| - 4 | - 9 | - 1 | - 5 | - 7 |

1. <u>Trace</u>. <u>Write</u> in the missing numbers. <u>Color</u> the rectangles.

10 + 4 = 14   fourteen fourteen

14	
0	
1	
2	
3	
4	
5	
6	
7	
8	
9	
10	
11	
12	
13	
14	

www.homerunpress.com

1. Write the missing numbers. Add or subtract.

$10 + 4 =$ __	$14 - 10 =$ __
$13 + 1 =$ __	$14 - 13 =$ __

$5 + 9 = 1 + 9 + 4 =$ __ $14 - 5 = 14 - 4 - 1 =$ __
| | | | | |
1   4   4   1

$6 + 8 = 2 + \_ + \_ =$ __ $14 - 6 = 14 - \_ - \_ =$ __
| | | | | |
2   4   4   2

$7 + 7 = \_ + \_ + \_ =$ __ $14 - 7 = \_ - \_ - \_ =$ __
| | | |
_   _   _   _

$8 + 6 = \_ + \_ + \_ =$ __ $14 - 8 = \_ - \_ - \_ =$ __
| | | |
_   _   _   _

$9 + 5 = \_ + \_ + \_ =$ __ $14 - 9 = \_ - \_ - \_ =$ __
| | | |
_   _   _   _

1. Write the missing numbers. Add or subtract.

$12 + 2 = \underline{}$

$14 - 12 = \underline{}$

$11 + 3 = \underline{}$

$14 - 11 = \underline{}$

$9 + 5 = 9 + \_ + \_ = \underline{}$

$14 - 7 = 14 - \_ - \_ = \underline{}$

$1 \quad \_$

$4 \quad \_$

$8 + 6 = \_ + \_ + \_ = \underline{}$

$14 - 9 = \_ - \_ - \_ = \underline{}$

$\_ \quad \_$

$\_ \quad \_$

$7 + 7 = \_ + \_ + \_ = \underline{}$

$14 - 5 = \_ - \_ - \_ = \underline{}$

$\_ \quad \_$

$\_ \quad \_$

$5 + 9 = \_ + \_ + \_ = \underline{}$

$14 - 6 = \_ - \_ - \_ = \underline{}$

$\_ \quad \_$

$\_ \quad \_$

$6 + 8 = \_ + \_ + \_ = \underline{}$

$14 - 7 = \_ - \_ - \_ = \underline{}$

$\_ \quad \_$

$\_ \quad \_$

www.homerunpress.com

1. <u>Write</u> the missing numbers. <u>Add</u> or <u>subtract</u>.

$4 + 10 =$ __ $14 - 4 =$ __

$3 + 11 =$ __ $14 - 3 =$ __

$7 + 6 = 7 + \_ + \_ =$ __ $14 - 7 = 14 - \_ - \_ =$ __

         3   _   4   _

$8 + 6 = \_ + \_ + \_ =$ __ $14 - 6 = \_ - \_ - \_ =$ __

$9 + 5 = \_ + \_ + \_ =$ __ $14 - 9 = \_ - \_ - \_ =$ __

$7 + 7 = \_ + \_ + \_ =$ __ $14 - 8 = \_ - \_ - \_ =$ __

$5 + 9 = \_ + \_ + \_ =$ __ $14 - 5 = \_ - \_ - \_ =$ __

1. <u>Write</u> the missing numbers. <u>Add</u> or <u>subtract</u>.

6 + 6 = __ + __ + __ = __   14 - 9 = __ - __ - __ = __

9 + 5 = __ + __ + __ = __   12 - 5 = __ - __ - __ = __

4 + 7 = __ + __ + __ = __   11 - 6 = __ - __ - __ = __

7 + 7 = __ + __ + __ = __   14 - 8 = __ - __ - __ = __

6 + 5 = __ + __ + __ = __   13 - 5 = __ - __ - __ = __

8 + 6 = __ + __ + __ = __   14 - 7 = __ - __ - __ = __

4 + 9 = __ + __ + __ = __   12 - 6 = __ - __ - __ = __

2. <u>Write</u> the missing numbers.

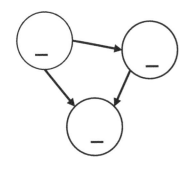

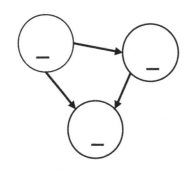

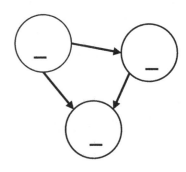

5, 11, 13   4, 7, 12   5, 9, 13

www.homerunpress.com

1. <u>Add.</u>

⁻5	⁻7	⁻3	1 2	⁻9
+ 9	+ 5	+ 8	+ 2	+ 2

⁻8	2	3	⁻5	⁻5
+ 6	+ 1 1	+ 1 0	+ 8	+ 9

1 0	⁻7	⁻8	⁻9	1 2
+ 4	+ 6	+ 6	+ 4	+ 1

2.

<u>Circle</u> the correct answer:

I have a series of numbers:

0, 2, 6, 8, 12, __

<u>What</u> is the next number?

A)   14   C)   13

B)   12   D)   11

1. <u>Write</u> the missing numbers. __ plus what equals __?

+ 8	+ 7	+ 9	+ 10	+ 6	+ 5
14	14	14	14	14	14

12	7	9	8	11	13
+	+	+	+	+	+
14	14	14	14	14	14

2. <u>Complete</u> each pair of number bonds.

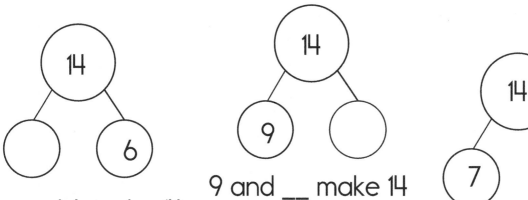

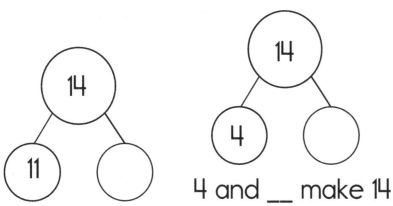

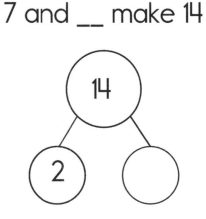

_ and 6 make 14

9 and __ make 14

7 and __ make 14

11 and __ make 14

4 and __ make 14

2 and __ make 14

www.homerunpress.com

1. <u>Subtract.</u>   Score ___/15   Time __:__

```
  0 14
  1 4      ‾1 ‾4      ‾1 ‾4      1 4      ‾1 ‾4
-   8     -   5     -   9     -   2     -   7
—————     —————     —————     —————     —————
    6
```

```
 ‾1 ‾4      1 4      1 4      ‾1 ‾4      ‾1 ‾4
-   6     -   1     -   4     -   8     -   5
—————     —————     —————     —————     —————
```

```
  1 4      ‾1 ‾4      1 4      ‾1 ‾4      ‾1 ‾4
-   4     -   7     -   3     -   9     -   6
—————     —————     —————     —————     —————
```

2.

Circle the correct answer:

I have a series of numbers:
0, 6, 3, 9, 6, 12, __.

<u>What</u> is the next number?

A)   10   C)   11

B)   12   D)   9

1. <u>Subtract.</u>

14	14	14	14	14
- 7	- 5	- 9	- 8	- 6

14	14	14	14	14
- 4	- 9	- 6	- 5	- 7

© 2020 Home Run Press, LLC www.homerunpress.com

1. <u>Trace</u>. <u>Write</u> in the missing numbers. <u>Color</u> the rectangles.

10 + 5 = 15   fifteen   fifteen

15	
0	
1	
2	
3	
4	
5	
6	
7	
8	
9	
10	
11	
12	
13	
14	
15	

1. Write the missing numbers. Add or subtract.

10 + 5 = __	15 - 10 = __
14 + 1 = __	15 - 14 = __

6 + 9 = 1 + 9 + 5 = __
| |
1 5
	15 - 6 = 15 - 5 - 1 = __
	  | |
	  5 1

7 + 8 = 2 + 8 + _ = __ | | 2 _	15 - 7 = 15 - 3 - _ = __ | | 5 _
8 + 7 = _ + _ + _ = __ | | _ _	15 - 8 = _ - _ - _ = __ | | _ _
9 + 5 = _ + _ + _ = __ | | _ _	15 - 9 = _ - _ - _ = __ | | _ _
9 + 6 = _ + _ + _ = __ | | _ _	15 - 8 = _ - _ - _ = __ | | _ _

1. Write the missing numbers. Add or subtract.

$12 + 3 =$ ___

$15 - 12 =$ ___

$13 + 2 =$ ___

$15 - 13 =$ ___

$9 + 6 =$ _ + _ + _ = ___

$15 - 6 = 1$_ - _ - _ = ___

$8 + 7 =$ _ + _ + _ = ___

$15 - 7 =$ _ - _ - _ = ___

$7 + 7 =$ _ + _ + _ = ___

$14 - 7 =$ _ - _ - _ = ___

$8 + 7 =$ _ + _ + _ = ___

$15 - 8 =$ _ - _ - _ = ___

$6 + 9 =$ _ + _ + _ = ___

$15 - 9 =$ _ - _ - _ = ___

1. <u>Write</u> the missing numbers. <u>Add</u> or <u>subtract</u>.

$4 + 11 = $ __

$15 - 4 = $ __

$2 + 13 = $ __

$15 - 2 = $ __

$6 + 5 = $ _ + _ + _ = __

$12 - 6 = $ _ - _ - _ = __

$8 + 3 = $ _ + _ + _ = __

$14 - 6 = $ _ - _ - _ = __

$7 + 5 = $ _ + _ + _ = __

$11 - 9 = $ _ - _ - _ = __

$6 + 9 = $ _ + _ + _ = __

$14 - 7 = $ _ - _ - _ = __

$6 + 6 = $ _ + _ + _ = __

$11 - 6 = $ _ - _ - _ = __

1. <u>Write</u> the missing numbers. <u>Add</u> or <u>subtract</u>.

8 + 7 = __ + __ + __ = __   15 - 9 = __ - __ - __ = __

9 + 2 = __ + __ + __ = __   14 - 5 = __ - __ - __ = __

3 + 8 = __ + __ + __ = __   12 - 6 = __ - __ - __ = __

6 + 7 = __ + __ + __ = __   13 - 8 = __ - __ - __ = __

9 + 6 = __ + __ + __ = __   11 - 5 = __ - __ - __ = __

5 + 6 = __ + __ + __ = __   12 - 7 = __ - __ - __ = __

4 + 8 = __ + __ + __ = __   14 - 6 = __ - __ - __ = __

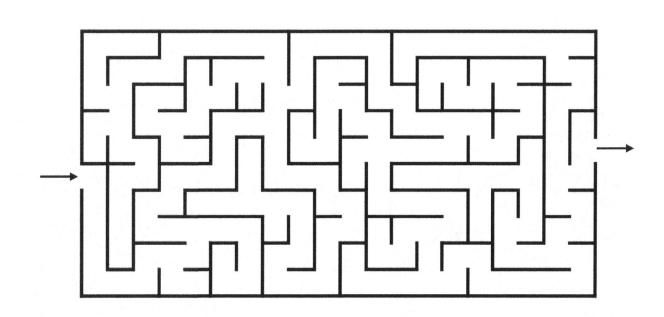

1. <u>Write</u> the missing numbers. __ plus what equals __?

```
    ‾ 6       ‾ 7       ‾ 5       ‾ 6       ‾ 9
  +   9     +   7     +   8     +   6     +   3
  _____   _____   _____   _____   _____
```

```
    ‾ 7         4         2       ‾ 6       ‾ 2
  +   5     + 1 1     + 1 2     +   7     +   9
  _____   _____   _____   _____   _____
```

```
    1 0       ‾ 7       ‾ 8       ‾ 9       1 2
  +   5     +   8     +   4     +   6     +   3
  _____   _____   _____   _____   _____
```

2.

Circle the correct answer:

I have a series of numbers:

0, 5, 10, __

<u>What</u> is the next number?

A) 14   C) 20

B) 12   D) 15

1. <u>Add</u>. <u>Write</u> the missing numbers.

7	6	6	5	8	9
+ 8	+ 6	+ 9	+ 10	+ 7	+ 6

12	7	9	7	11	2
+ 3	+ 8	+ 2	+ 5	+ 4	+ 13

2. <u>Complete</u> each pair of number bonds.

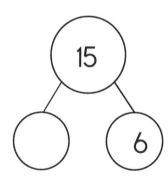

_ and 6 make 15

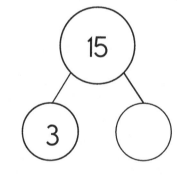

3 and __ make 15

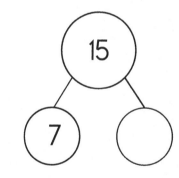

7 and __ make 15

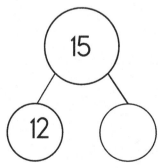

12 and __ make 15

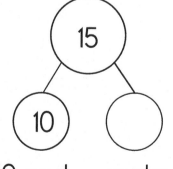

10 and __ make 15

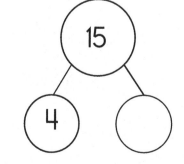

4 and __ make 15

1. Subtract.   Score ___/15   Time __:__

```
  0 15
  1̶ 5̶          1 5          1̄ 5̄          1 5          1̄ 5̄
-    8       -    5       -    9       -    2       -    7
─────        ─────        ─────        ─────        ─────
     7
```

```
  1̄ 5̄          1 5          1 5          1̄ 5̄          1 5
-    6       -    1       -    4       -    8       -    3
─────        ─────        ─────        ─────        ─────
```

```
  1̄ 4̄          1̄ 1̄          1̄ 2̄          1̄ 1̄          1̄ 5̄
-    8       -    7       -    3       -    9       -    6
─────        ─────        ─────        ─────        ─────
```

2.

Circle the correct answer:

I have a series of numbers:
0, 3, 6, 9, __, 15.

What is the missing number?

A)   10   C)   11

B)   12   D)   9

       www.homerunpress.com

1. Subtract.

15	11	12	14	15
− 7	− 5	− 3	− 8	− 6

15	15	15	11	15
− 4	− 9	− 3	− 7	− 7

© 2020 Home Run Press, LLC

1. Trace. Write in the missing numbers. Color the rectangles.

10 + 6 = 16   sixteen   sixteen

16	
0	
1	
2	
3	
4	
5	
6	
7	
8	
9	
10	
11	
12	
13	
14	
15	
16	

1. <u>Write</u> the missing numbers. Add or subtract.

$10 + 6 =$ __ | $16 - 10 =$ __

$15 + 1 =$ __ | $16 - 15 =$ __

$7 + 9 = 1 + \_ + \_ =$ __ | $16 - 7 = \_ - \_ - \_ =$ __

    | | | | |

1 6 | 6 1

$8 + 8 = \_ + \_ + \_ =$ __ | $16 - 8 = \_ - \_ - \_ =$ __

$4 + 7 = \_ + \_ + \_ =$ __ | $12 - 9 = \_ - \_ - \_ =$ __

$5 + 8 = \_ + \_ + \_ =$ __ | $15 - 7 = \_ - \_ - \_ =$ __

$8 + 3 = \_ + \_ + \_ =$ __ | $12 - 8 = \_ - \_ - \_ =$ __

1. <u>Write</u> the missing numbers. Add or subtract.

11 + 5 = __   16 - 11 = __

4 + 12 = __   16 - 13 = __

9 + 7 = _ + _ + _ = __   15 - 7 = _ - _ - _ = __
    | | | |
    1   _   5   _

8 + 7 = _ + _ + _ = __   14 - 8 = _ - _ - _ = __
    | | | |
  _   _   _   _

9 + 3 = _ + _ + _ = __   11 - 7 = _ - _ - _ = __
    | | | |
  _   _   _   _

6 + 7 = _ + _ + _ = __   12 - 5 = _ - _ - _ = __
  | | | |
 _   _   _   _

4 + 9 = _ + _ + _ = __   15 - 6 = _ - _ - _ = __
  | | | |
 _   _   _   _

1. <u>Write</u> the missing numbers. Add or subtract.

$3 + 13 = \_\_$ $16 - 3 = \_\_$

$1 + 15 = \_\_$ $16 - 2 = \_\_$

$9 + 6 = \_ + \_ + \_ = \_\_$ $16 - 7 = \_ - \_ - \_ = \_\_$

$7 + 4 = \_ + \_ + \_ = \_\_$ $12 - 6 = \_ - \_ - \_ = \_\_$

$9 + 5 = \_ + \_ + \_ = \_\_$ $14 - 9 = \_ - \_ - \_ = \_\_$

$6 + 7 = \_ + \_ + \_ = \_\_$ $12 - 8 = \_ - \_ - \_ = \_\_$

$5 + 8 = \_ + \_ + \_ = \_\_$ $11 - 4 = \_ - \_ - \_ = \_\_$

1. <u>Write</u> the missing numbers. Add or subtract.

8 + 4 = __ + __ + __ = __   12 - 9 = __ - __ - __ = __

9 + 7 = __ + __ + __ = __   11 - 5 = __ - __ - __ = __

5 + 8 = __ + __ + __ = __   14 - 6 = __ - __ - __ = __

6 + 9 = __ + __ + __ = __   16 - 8 = __ - __ - __ = __

9 + 3 = __ + __ + __ = __   13 - 5 = __ - __ - __ = __

5 + 7 = __ + __ + __ = __   16 - 7 = __ - __ - __ = __

8 + 8 = __ + __ + __ = __   12 - 6 = __ - __ - __ = __

2. Write the missing numbers. The arrow means: __ is

greater than __.

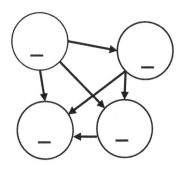 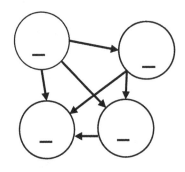 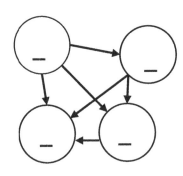

10, 8, 14, 3   6, 15, 9, 13   12, 16, 14, 7

                  www.homerunpress.com

1. <u>Add.</u>

⁻7	⁻6	⁻5	⁻7	⁻8
+ 9	+ 7	+ 9	+ 7	+ 4

⁻8	2	3	⁻6	⁻4
+ 8	+ 1 4	+ 1 3	+ 7	+ 7

1 1	1 0	⁻8	⁻9	1 2
+ 3	+ 6	+ 7	+ 7	+ 4

2.

Circle the correct answer:

I have a series of numbers:
0, 4, 8, 12, __

What is the next number?

A) 20   C) 13

B) 14   D) 16

1. Add.

```
    8          6          3          3          8          9
 +  8       +  9       +  9       + 13       +  4       +  7
_____    _____    _____    _____    _____    _____
```

```
   12          7          9          8         11          1
 +  4       +  7       +  2       +  5       +  5       + 15
_____    _____    _____    _____    _____    _____
```

2. Complete each pair of number bonds.

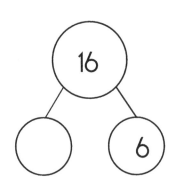

_ and 6 make 16

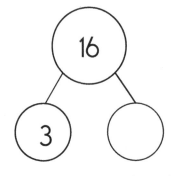

3 and __ make 16

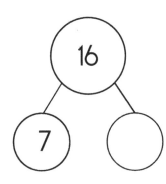

7 and __ make 16

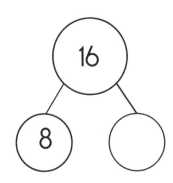

8 and __ make 13

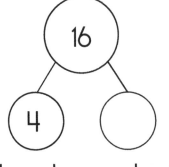

4 and __ make 16

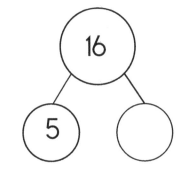

5 and __ make 16

www.homerunpress.com

1. Subtract.   Score ___/15   Time __:__

```
  0 16
  1̶ 6̶          1 6          ¯1̄ ¯6̄         1 6          ¯1̄ ¯6̄
-    8        -   5        -   9        - 1 2        -   7
─────        ─────        ─────        ─────        ─────
     8
```

```
  1 6          1 6          1 6          ¯1̄ ¯6̄         1 6̄
- 1 6        - 1 1        -   4        -   8        -   5
─────        ─────        ─────        ─────        ─────
```

```
 ¯1̄ ¯2̄         ¯1̄ ¯4̄         ¯1̄ ¯1̄         ¯1̄ ¯5̄         ¯1̄ ¯3̄
-    4        -   7        -   3        -   9        -   6
─────        ─────        ─────        ─────        ─────
```

2.

Circle the correct answer:

I have a series of numbers:
0, 2, 5, 9, __.

What is the next number?

A)   10   C)   11
B)   12   D)   14

1. <u>Subtract.</u>

16	16	16	16	16
− 7	− 5	− 3	− 8	− 6

16	16	16	16	16
− 14	− 9	− 1	− 15	− 7

1. Trace. Write in the missing numbers. Color the rectangles.

10 + 7 = 17   seventeen seventeen

17	
0	
1	
2	
3	
4	
5	
6	
7	
8	
9	
10	
11	
12	
13	
14	
15	
16	
17	

1. <u>Write</u> the missing numbers. <u>Add</u> or <u>subtract</u>.

10 + 7 = __   17 - 10 = __

16 + 1 = __   17 - 16 = __

8 + 9 = 1 + 9 + _ = __   17 - 8 = _ - _ - _ = __
| | | |
1 7   7 1

3 + 9 = _ + _ + _ = __   16 - 7 = _ - _ - _ = __
| | | |
_ _   _ _

7 + 7 = _ + _ + _ = __   12 - 6 = _ - _ - _ = __
| | | |
_ _   _ _

5 + 8 = _ + _ + _ = __   12 - 9 = _ - _ - _ = __
| | | |
_ _   _ _

9 + 4 = _ + _ + _ = __   11 - 8 = _ - _ - _ = __
| | | |
_ _   _ _

1. <u>Write</u> the missing numbers. <u>Add</u> or <u>subtract</u>.

12 + 5 = __

4 + 13 = __

9 + 8 = 9 + _ + _ = __

1   _

8 + 5 = _ + _ + _ = __

_   _

9 + 7 = _ + _ + _ = __

_   _

6 + 7 = _ + _ + _ = __

_   _

6 + 9 = _ + _ + _ = __

_   _

17 - 12 = __

17 - 4 = __

14 - 6 = 14 - _ - _ = __

4   _

11 - 6 = _ - _ - _ = __

_   _

15 - 8 = _ - _ - _ = __

_   _

11 - 5 = _ - _ - _ = __

_   _

17 - 9 = _ - _ - _ = __

_   _

1. Write the missing numbers. Add or subtract.

8 + 8 = __ + __ + __ = __   15 - 9 = __ - __ - __ = __

9 + 8 = __ + __ + __ = __   14 - 5 = __ - __ - __ = __

5 + 6 = __ + __ + __ = __   13 - 6 = __ - __ - __ = __

6 + 7 = __ + __ + __ = __   17 - 8 = __ - __ - __ = __

9 + 4 = __ + __ + __ = __   11 - 5 = __ - __ - __ = __

7 + 7 = __ + __ + __ = __   13 - 9 = __ - __ - __ = __

6 + 8 = __ + __ + __ = __   12 - 6 = __ - __ - __ = __

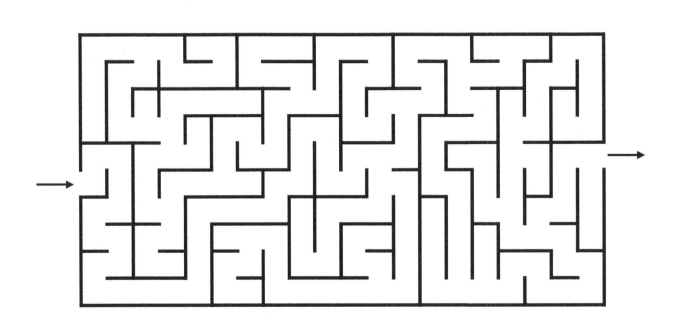

www.homerunpress.com

1. Add.

$$
\begin{array}{r} ^-6 \\ +\ 9 \\ \hline \end{array}
\qquad
\begin{array}{r} ^-6 \\ +\ 6 \\ \hline \end{array}
\qquad
\begin{array}{r} ^-9 \\ +\ 8 \\ \hline \end{array}
\qquad
\begin{array}{r} ^-6 \\ +\ 7 \\ \hline \end{array}
\qquad
\begin{array}{r} ^-9 \\ +\ 5 \\ \hline \end{array}
$$

$$
\begin{array}{r} ^-8 \\ +\ 8 \\ \hline \end{array}
\qquad
\begin{array}{r} 6 \\ +11 \\ \hline \end{array}
\qquad
\begin{array}{r} 3 \\ +14 \\ \hline \end{array}
\qquad
\begin{array}{r} 6 \\ +10 \\ \hline \end{array}
\qquad
\begin{array}{r} ^-2 \\ +\ 9 \\ \hline \end{array}
$$

$$
\begin{array}{r} 12 \\ +\ 3 \\ \hline \end{array}
\qquad
\begin{array}{r} ^-7 \\ +\ 7 \\ \hline \end{array}
\qquad
\begin{array}{r} ^-8 \\ +\ 9 \\ \hline \end{array}
\qquad
\begin{array}{r} ^-9 \\ +\ 5 \\ \hline \end{array}
\qquad
\begin{array}{r} 12 \\ +\ 2 \\ \hline \end{array}
$$

2.

Circle the correct answer:

I have a series of numbers:

0, 3, 8, __

What is the next number?

A) 14   C) 15

B) 17   D) 13

1. <u>Add</u>.

9 + 8	6 + 6	5 + 9	3 + 14	8 + 8	9 + 7

12 + 5	7 + 8	9 + 3	8 + 7	11 + 6	3 + 13

2. <u>Complete</u> each pair of number bonds.

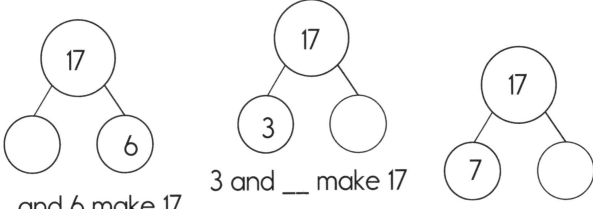

_ and 6 make 17

3 and __ make 17

7 and __ make 17

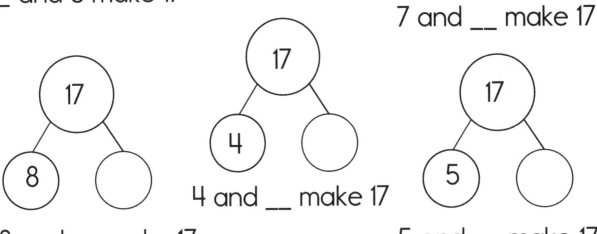

8 and __ make 17

4 and __ make 17

5 and __ make 17

1. <u>Subtract.</u>   Score ___/15   Time __:__

```
  0 17
  1̶ 7̶        1 7       1̶ 7̶       1 7       1 7
-   8       -   5      -   9     -   2      -   7
─────       ─────      ─────     ─────      ─────
    9
```

```
  1 7       1 7       1 7       1̶ 7̶       1 7
- 1 6       -   1     - 1 4     -   8     - 1 5
─────       ─────     ─────     ─────     ─────
```

```
  1 7       1 7       1 7       1̶ 7̶       1 7
-   4       - 1 7     -   3     -   9     - 1 6
─────       ─────     ─────     ─────     ─────
```

2.

Circle the correct answer:

I have a series of numbers:
7, 9, 11, 13, 15, __.

<u>What</u> is the next number?

A)   16   C)   17
B)   15   D)   14

1. Subtract.

17 − 7	17 − 5	17 − 3	17 − 8	17 − 6

17 − 14	17 − 9	17 − 11	17 − 15	17 − 17

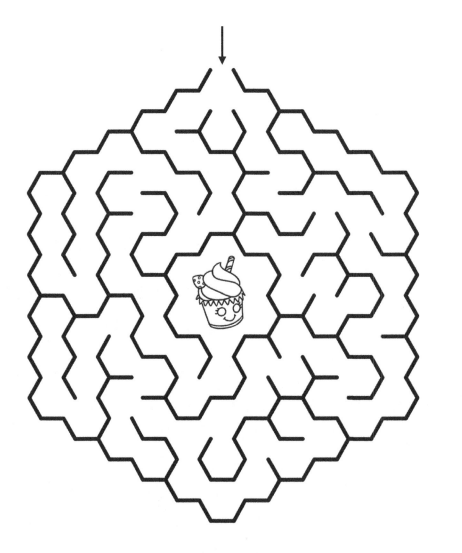

1. Trace. Write in the missing numbers. Color the rectangles.

10 + 8 = 18   eighteen   eighteen

18	
0	
1	
2	
3	
4	
5	
6	
7	
8	
9	
10	
11	
12	
13	
14	
15	
16	
17	
18	

1. Write the missing numbers. Add or subtract.

$10 + 8 =$ __

$18 - 0 =$ __

$17 + 1 =$ __

$18 - 17 =$ __

$9 + 9 = 9 + \_ + \_ =$ __

$18 - 9 = 18 - \_ - \_ =$ __

1 _

8 _

$8 + 7 = \_ + \_ + \_ =$ __

$17 - 8 = \_ - \_ - \_ =$ __

_ _

_ _

$9 + 6 = \_ + \_ + \_ =$ __

$14 - 7 = \_ - \_ - \_ =$ __

_ _

_ _

$5 + 8 = \_ + \_ + \_ =$ __

$15 - 9 = \_ - \_ - \_ =$ __

_ _

_ _

$4 + 7 = \_ + \_ + \_ =$ __

$13 - 7 = \_ - \_ - \_ =$ __

_ _

_ _

www.homerunpress.com

1. Write the missing numbers. Add or subtract.

13 + 5 = __	18 - 7 = __
12 + 6 = __	18 - 14 = __
8 + 6 = _ + _ + _ = __	16 - 8 = _ - _ - _ = __
9 + 7 = _ + _ + _ = __	14 - 8 = _ - _ - _ = __
6 + 5 = _ + _ + _ = __	11 - 9 = _ - _ - _ = __
8 + 9 = _ + _ + _ = __	13 - 4 = _ - _ - _ = __
9 + 9 = _ + _ + _ = __	17 - 8 = _ - _ - _ = __

1. <u>Write</u> the missing numbers. <u>Add</u> or <u>subtract</u>.

8 + 7 = __ + __ + __ = __   17 - 9 = __ - __ - __ = __

9 + 9 = __ + __ + __ = __   14 - 7 = __ - __ - __ = __

6 + 8 = __ + __ + __ = __   16 - 8 = __ - __ - __ = __

7 + 9 = __ + __ + __ = __   15 - 7 = __ - __ - __ = __

8 + 3 = __ + __ + __ = __   11 - 5 = __ - __ - __ = __

5 + 6 = __ + __ + __ = __   13 - 7 = __ - __ - __ = __

8 + 8 = __ + __ + __ = __   16 - 9 = __ - __ - __ = __

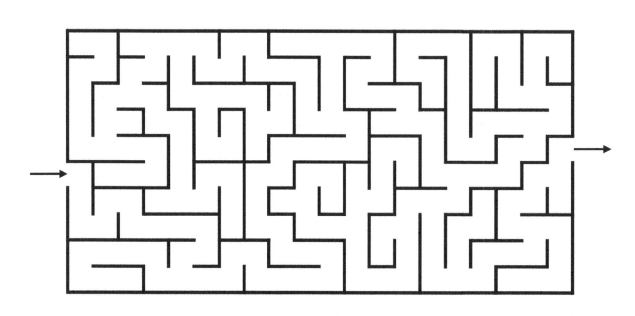

     www.homerunpress.com

1. <u>Add.</u>

9	5	6	9	9
+ 9	+ 7	+ 8	+ 7	+ 3

8	2	3	6	8
+ 4	+ 9	+ 8	+ 6	+ 9

4	7	8	9	7
+ 9	+ 7	+ 8	+ 6	+ 6

2.

Circle the correct answer:

I have a series of numbers:
0, 6, 12, __

What is the next number?

A)   15   C)   18
B)   16   D)   17

1. <u>Subtract.</u>   Score ___/15   Time __:__

$$\begin{array}{r} 0\ 18 \\ \cancel{1}\ \cancel{8} \\ -\quad 9 \\ \hline \end{array}$$
$$\begin{array}{r} 1\ 8 \\ -\ 1\ 5 \\ \hline \end{array}$$
$$\begin{array}{r} 1\ 8 \\ -\ 1\ 1 \\ \hline \end{array}$$
$$\begin{array}{r} 1\ 8 \\ -\quad 2 \\ \hline \end{array}$$
$$\begin{array}{r} 1\ 8 \\ -\quad 7 \\ \hline \end{array}$$

$$\begin{array}{r} 1\ 8 \\ -\quad 6 \\ \hline \end{array}$$
$$\begin{array}{r} 1\ 8 \\ -\quad 1 \\ \hline \end{array}$$
$$\begin{array}{r} 1\ 8 \\ -\quad 4 \\ \hline \end{array}$$
$$\begin{array}{r} 1\ 8 \\ -\quad 8 \\ \hline \end{array}$$
$$\begin{array}{r} 1\ 8 \\ -\quad 5 \\ \hline \end{array}$$

$$\begin{array}{r} 1\ 8 \\ -\ 1\ 4 \\ \hline \end{array}$$
$$\begin{array}{r} 1\ 8 \\ -\ 1\ 7 \\ \hline \end{array}$$
$$\begin{array}{r} 1\ 8 \\ -\quad 3 \\ \hline \end{array}$$
$$\begin{array}{r} \overline{1}\ \overline{8} \\ -\quad 9 \\ \hline \end{array}$$
$$\begin{array}{r} 1\ 8 \\ -\ 1\ 6 \\ \hline \end{array}$$

2.

Circle the correct answer:

I have a series of numbers:
0, 4, 10, __.

<u>What</u> is the next number?

A)   18   C)   17
B)   16   D)   15

www.homerunpress.com

1. Trace. Write in the missing numbers. Color the rectangles.

10 + 9 = 19   nineteen nineteen

19	
0	
1	
2	
3	
4	
5	
6	
7	
8	
9	
10	
11	
12	
13	
14	
15	
16	
17	
18	
19	

1. <u>Write</u> the missing numbers. <u>Add</u> or <u>subtract</u>.

8 + 8 = __ + __ + __ = __   18 - 9 = __ - __ - __ = __

9 + 9 = __ + __ + __ = __   13 - 5 = __ - __ - __ = __

5 + 6 = __ + __ + __ = __   14 - 8 = __ - __ - __ = __

6 + 7 = __ + __ + __ = __   16 - 9 = __ - __ - __ = __

9 + 4 = __ + __ + __ = __   13 - 7 = __ - __ - __ = __

7 + 7 = __ + __ + __ = __   16 - 9 = __ - __ - __ = __

8 + 3 = __ + __ + __ = __   12 - 7 = __ - __ - __ = __

2. <u>Draw</u> the missing arrows. The arrow means: __ is greater than __.

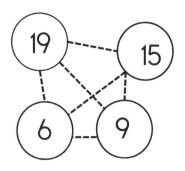

6, 9, 15, 19

2, 4, 13, 16

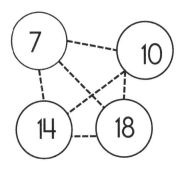

7, 10, 14, 18

1. <u>Add</u>. <u>Write</u> the missing numbers.

1 1	1 6	1 5	1 6	1 9
+	+	+	+	+
1 9	1 9	1 9	1 9	1 9

1 8		1 3	1 4	1 0
+	+ 1 7	+	+	+
1 9	1 9	1 9	1 9	1 9

− 9	− 7	− 8	− 6	− 7
+ 3	+ 8	+ 4	+ 6	+ 7

2.

Circle the correct answer:

I have a series of numbers:
3, 4, 7, 12, __

<u>What</u> is the next number?

A)   18   C)   15

B)   19   D)   17

1. <u>Subtract.</u>   Score ___/15   Time __:__

```
  1 9        1 9        1 9        1 9        1 9
-   8      -   5      -   9      -   2      -   7
─────
  1 1
```

```
  1 9        1 9        1 9        1 9        1 9
-   6      -   1      -   4      - 1 8      - 1 5
```

```
  1 9        1 9        1 9        1 9        1 9
- 1 4      - 1 7      - 1 3      - 1 9      - 1 6
```

2.

Circle the correct answer:

I have a series of numbers:
1, 5, 9, 13, __.

<u>What</u> is the next number?

A)   15   C)   16
B)   17   D)   19

              www.homerunpress.com

1. Trace. Write in the missing numbers. Color the rectangles.

10 + 10 = 20   twenty   twenty

20	
0	
1	
2	
3	
4	
5	
6	
7	
8	
9	
10	
11	
12	
13	
14	
15	
16	
17	
18	
19	
20	

1. <u>Write</u> the missing numbers. <u>Add</u> or <u>subtract</u>.

14 + 6 =   10+4+6= __
| |
10   4

20 - 14 = 10 +10 -10 -4 = __
| |
10   10

15 + 5 = 10+5+ _ = __
| |
10   5

20 - 5 = 10+10-5   = __
| |
10   10

11 + 9 = 10+ _ + _ = __
| |
10   _

20 - 16 = _ + _ - _ - _ = __
| |
_   _

18 + 2 = _ + _ + _ = __
| |
_   _

20 - 11 = _ + _ - _ - _ = __
| |
_   _

3 + 17 = _ + _ + _ = __
| |
_   _

20 - 8 = _ + _ - _ = __
| |
_   _

12 + 8 = _ + _ + _ = __
| |
_   _

20 - 13 = _ + _ - _ - _ = __
| |
_   _

19 + 1 = _ + _ + _ = __
| |
_   _

20 - 4 = _ + _ - _ - _ = __
| |
_   _

www.homerunpress.com

1. Write the missing numbers. Add or subtract.

13 + 7 = 10+ _ + _ = __
| |
10 _

20 - 15 = _ + _ - _ - _ = __
| |
10 _

5 + 15 = _ + _ + _ = __
| |
_ _

20 - 2 = _ + _ - _ = __
| |
_ _

17 + 3 = _ + _ + _ = __
| |
_ _

20 - 19 = _ + _ - _ - _ = __
| |
_ _

16 + 4 = _ + _ + _ = __
| |
_ _

20 - 4 = _ + _ - _ = __
| |
_ _

1 + 19 = _ + _ + _ = __
| |
_ _

20 - 8 = _ + _ - _ = __
| |
_ _

7 + 13 = _ + _ + _ = __
| |
_ _

20 - 17 = _ + _ - _ - _ = __
| |
_ _

8 + 12 = _ + _ + _ = __
| |
_ _

20 - 9 = _ + _ - _ = __
| |
_ _

1. Write the missing numbers. Add or subtract.

$9 + 11 = \_ + \_ + \_ = \_\_$

$20 - 12 = \_ + \_ - \_ - \_ = \_\_$

10　　_

$6 + 14 = \_ + \_ + \_ = \_\_$

$20 - 7 = \_ + \_ - \_ = \_\_$

$8 + 9 = \_ + \_ + \_ = \_\_$

$20 - 1 = \_ + \_ - \_ - \_ = \_\_$

$6 + 9 = \_ + \_ + \_ = \_\_$

$20 - 18 = \_ + \_ - \_ = \_\_$

$9 + 5 = \_ + \_ + \_ = \_\_$

$20 - 6 = \_ + \_ - \_ = \_\_$

$9 + 7 = \_ + \_ + \_ = \_\_$

$20 - 3 = \_ + \_ - \_ = \_\_$

$9 + 6 = \_ + \_ + \_ = \_\_$

$20 - 7 = \_ + \_ - \_ = \_\_$

1. <u>Write</u> the missing numbers. <u>Add</u> or <u>subtract</u>.

14 + 6 = __ + __ + __ = __   20 - 9 = __ + __ - __ = __

19 + 1 = __ + __ + __ = __   20 - 5 = __ - __ - __ = __

15 + 5 = __ + __ + __ = __   20 - 6 = __ - __ - __ = __

16 + 4 = __ + __ + __ = __   20 - 8 = __ - __ - __ = __

17 + 3 = __ + __ + __ = __   20 - 1 = __ - __ - __ = __

12 + 8 = __ + __ + __ = __   20 - 7 = __ - __ - __ = __

13 + 7 = __ + __ + __ = __   20 - 3 = __ - __ - __ = __

1. <u>Write</u> the missing numbers. __ plus what equals __?

$$
\begin{array}{r} 1\ 1 \\ +\ \underline{} \\ 2\ 0 \end{array} \qquad
\begin{array}{r} 1\ 6 \\ +\ \underline{} \\ 2\ 0 \end{array} \qquad
\begin{array}{r} 1\ 5 \\ +\ \underline{} \\ 2\ 0 \end{array} \qquad
\begin{array}{r} 1\ 2 \\ +\ \underline{} \\ 2\ 0 \end{array} \qquad
\begin{array}{r} 1\ 9 \\ +\ \underline{} \\ 2\ 0 \end{array}
$$

$$
\begin{array}{r} +\ 1\ 2 \\ \hline 2\ 0 \end{array} \qquad
\begin{array}{r} +\ 1\ 1 \\ \hline 2\ 0 \end{array} \qquad
\begin{array}{r} +\ 1\ 7 \\ \hline 2\ 0 \end{array} \qquad
\begin{array}{r} +\ 1\ 4 \\ \hline 2\ 0 \end{array} \qquad
\begin{array}{r} +\ 1\ 9 \\ \hline 2\ 0 \end{array}
$$

$$
\begin{array}{r} 1\ 7 \\ +\ \underline{} \\ 2\ 0 \end{array} \qquad
\begin{array}{r} +\ 1\ 6 \\ \hline 2\ 0 \end{array} \qquad
\begin{array}{r} 1\ 8 \\ +\ \underline{} \\ 2\ 0 \end{array} \qquad
\begin{array}{r} 1\ 9 \\ +\ \underline{} \\ 2\ 0 \end{array} \qquad
\begin{array}{r} 1\ 2 \\ +\ \underline{} \\ 2\ 0 \end{array}
$$

2.

<u>Circle</u> the correct answer:

I have a series of numbers:
5, 10, 15, __

<u>What</u> is the next number?

A) 16   C) 20

B) 22   D) 25

1. <u>Write</u> the missing numbers. __ plus what equals __?

```
   12              14              5
+            +  7   +          + 17   +          + 11
─────       ─────   ─────      ─────   ─────      ─────
  20          20      20         20      20         20


   12              16             18
+            + 13    +          +  5   +          +  7
─────       ─────   ─────      ─────   ─────      ─────
  20          20      20         20      20         20
```

2. <u>Complete</u> each pair of number bonds.

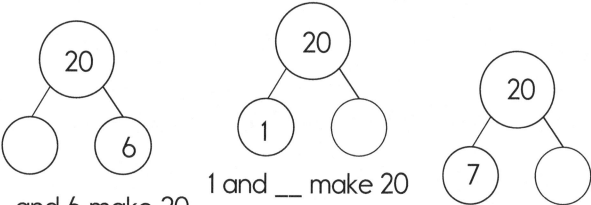

_ and 6 make 20

1 and __ make 20

7 and __ make 20

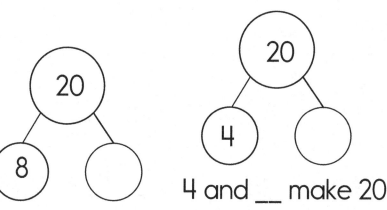

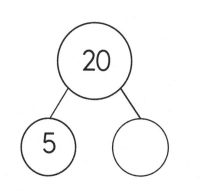

8 and __ make 20

4 and __ make 20

5 and __ make 20

1. <u>Write</u> the missing numbers.

2 + 18 = __ + __ + __ = __   20 - 12 = __ + __ - __ - _ = __

7 + 13 = __ + __ + __ = __   20 - 17 = __ + __ - __ - _ = __

6 + 14 = __ + __ + __ = __   20 - 11 = __ + __ - __ - _ = __

8 + 12 = __ + __ + __ = __   20 - 18 = __ + __ - __ - _ = __

9 + 11 = __ + __ + __ = __   20 - 14 = __ + __ - __ - _ = __

5 + 15 = __ + __ + __ = __   20 - 19 = __ + __ - __ - _ = __

1 + 19 = __ + __ + __ = __   20 - 15 = __ + __ - __ - _ = __

2. <u>Draw</u> the missing arrows. The arrow means: __ is greater than __.

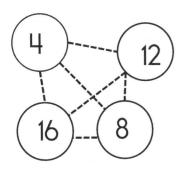

4, 8, 12, 16

9, 12, 15, 18

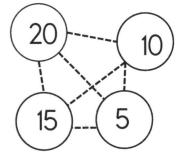

5, 10, 15, 20

1. Subtract.   Score ___/15   Time __:__

```
  1 10        ‾ ‾        ‾ ‾        ‾ ‾        ‾ ‾
  2 0         2 0        2 0        2 0        2 0
- 1 8       - 1 5      - 1 9      - 1 2      - 1 7
---------   ---------  ---------  ---------  ---------
    2
```

```
  ‾ ‾        ‾ ‾        ‾ ‾        ‾ ‾        ‾ ‾
  2 0        2 0        2 0        2 0        2 0
- 1 6      - 1 1      - 1 4      - 1 8      - 1 5
---------  ---------  ---------  ---------  ---------
```

```
  ‾ ‾        ‾ ‾        ‾ ‾        ‾ ‾        ‾ ‾
  2 0        2 0        2 0        2 0        2 0
- 1 5      - 1 7      - 1 3      - 1 9      - 1 6
---------  ---------  ---------  ---------  ---------
```

2.

Circle the correct answer:

I have a series of numbers:

1, 5, 11, __.

What is the next number?

A) 15   C) 19
B) 16   D) 20

1. Subtract.

$$
\begin{array}{r} 20 \\ -\ \ 7 \\ \hline \end{array}
\qquad
\begin{array}{r} 20 \\ -\ \ 5 \\ \hline \end{array}
\qquad
\begin{array}{r} 20 \\ -\ \ 3 \\ \hline \end{array}
\qquad
\begin{array}{r} 20 \\ -\ \ 8 \\ \hline \end{array}
\qquad
\begin{array}{r} 20 \\ -\ \ 6 \\ \hline \end{array}
$$

$$
\begin{array}{r} 20 \\ -\ \ 4 \\ \hline \end{array}
\qquad
\begin{array}{r} 20 \\ -\ \ 9 \\ \hline \end{array}
\qquad
\begin{array}{r} 20 \\ -\ \ 1 \\ \hline \end{array}
\qquad
\begin{array}{r} 20 \\ -\ \ 5 \\ \hline \end{array}
\qquad
\begin{array}{r} 20 \\ -\ \ 7 \\ \hline \end{array}
$$

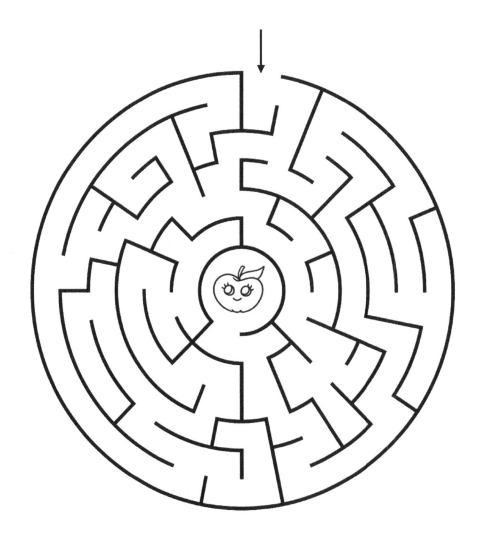

www.homerunpress.com

1. <u>Complete</u> an addition number sentence with tens and ones.

$10 = 10 + 0$ $11 = \_\_ + \_\_$ $12 = \_\_ + \_\_$

$13 = \_\_ + \_\_$ $14 = \_\_ + \_\_$ $15 = \_\_ + \_\_$

$16 = \_\_ + \_\_$ $17 = \_\_ + \_\_$ $18 = \_\_ + \_\_$

$19 = \_\_ + \_\_$ $20 = \_\_ + \_\_$ $21 = \_\_ + \_\_$

$22 = \_\_ + \_\_$ $23 = \_\_ + \_\_$ $24 = \_\_ + \_\_$

$25 = \_\_ + \_\_$ $26 = \_\_ + \_\_$ $27 = \_\_ + \_\_$

$28 = \_\_ + \_\_$ $29 = \_\_ + \_\_$ $30 = \_\_ + \_\_$

$31 = \_\_ + \_\_$ $32 = \_\_ + \_\_$ $33 = \_\_ + \_\_$

$34 = \_\_ + \_\_$ $35 = \_\_ + \_\_$ $36 = \_\_ + \_\_$

$37 = \_\_ + \_\_$ $38 = \_\_ + \_\_$ $39 = \_\_ + \_\_$

Panel (top-left) — Write the missing numbers.

1. Write the missing numbers.

0 + 11 = 11	11 - 0 = 11
1 + 10 = 11	11 - 1 = 10
2 + 9 = 1+9+1=11	11 - 2 = 11-1-1 = 9
3 + 8 = 2+8+1=11	11 - 3 = 11-1-2 = 8
4 + 7 = 3+7+1=11	11 - 4 = 11-1-3 = 7
5 + 6 = 4+6+1=11	11 - 5 = 11-1-4 = 6
6 + 5 = 6+4+1=11	11 - 6 = 11-1-5 = 5

Panel (top-right) — carry over

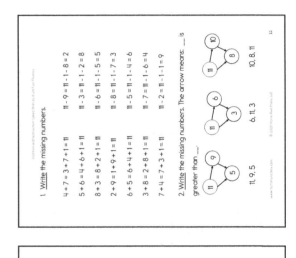

1) Write ones under ones.
2) Carry over when the sum is 10 or more.
3) Find out how many more you need to add to a greater number to get a ten.

Step 1: I need one more row above 8 to write the numbers that were carried over.

Step 2: First, I add ones: 8+3=8+2+1=11. I created a whole new ten, and it will go in the tens column.

Write the 1 in one's place. Carry 1 ten with the tens. Write the 1 in the ten's column.

Step 3: Add up the tens column: 1+0+0=1

Panel (row 2, left) — First, make ten

3 + 8
2   1

First, make ten! I need to add two more to 8 to get 10. So, I decompose a smaller number.

3 is 2+1

I take "2" out of the "3" and put "2" to the "8": 2 + 8

Now I have 10 and "1" leftover: 10 + 1 = 11

So, 3 + 8 is the same thing as 10 + 1

Answer: 2 + 8 + 1 = 10 + 1 = 11

I need to subtract 9 ones out of 11 ones. I decompose 9. 9 is 1 + 8.

First I take away 1 out of 11 to make 10. But to take away a total of 9, I have to take away 8 more.

11 - 1 - 8 = 10 - 8 = 2

Panel (row 2, right) — Write the missing numbers.

1. Write the missing numbers.

4 + 7 = 3 + 7 + 1 = 11	11 - 9 = 11 - 8 = 2
5 + 6 = 4 + 6 + 1 = 11	11 - 3 = 11 - 1 - 2 = 8
8 + 3 = 8 + 2 + 1 = 11	11 - 6 = 11 - 1 - 5 = 5
2 + 9 = 1 + 9 + 1 = 11	11 - 8 = 11 - 1 - 7 = 3
6 + 5 = 6 + 4 + 1 = 11	11 - 5 = 11 - 1 - 4 = 6
3 + 8 = 2 + 8 + 1 = 11	11 - 7 = 11 - 1 - 6 = 4
7 + 4 = 7 + 3 + 1 = 11	11 - 2 = 11 - 1 - 1 = 9

2. Write the missing numbers. The arrow means: ___ is greater than ___.

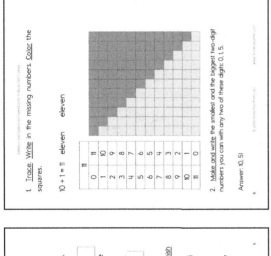

11, 9, 5   6, 11, 3   10, 8, 11

Panel (row 3, left) — Trace. Write the missing numbers.

1. Trace. Write in the missing numbers. Color the squares.

10 + 1 = 11   eleven   eleven

0	11
1	10
2	9
3	8
4	7
5	6
6	5
7	4
8	3
9	2
10	1
11	

2. Make and write the smallest and the biggest two-digit numbers you can with any two of these digits: 0, 1, 5.

Answer: 10, 51

Panel (row 3, right) — Write the missing numbers.

1. Write the missing numbers.

1 + 10 = 11	11 - 1 = 10
10 + 1 = 11	11 - 10 = 1
2 + 9 = 1+9+1=11	11 - 6 = 11-1-5 = 5
3 + 8 = 2+8+1=11	11 - 8 = 11-1-7 = 3
5 + 6 = 4+6+1=11	11 - 3 = 11-1-2 = 8
4 + 7 = 3+7+1=11	11 - 2 = 11-1-1 = 9
7 + 4 = 7+3+1=11	11 - 5 = 11-1-4 = 6

Panel (bottom-left) — Write the numbers

1. Write the numbers from 0 to 10.

0 1 2 3 4 5 6 7 8 9 10

2. Write these numerals. Trace the number words.

0	1	2	3	4	5
zero	one	two	three	four	five

6	7	8	9	10
six	seven	eight	nine	ten

3. Join the numbers with a line. Start at 0 and finish at 10.

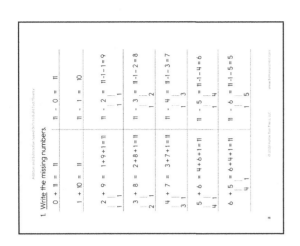

Panel (bottom-right) — Write the missing numbers.

1. Write the missing numbers.

11 + 0 = 11	11 - 11 = 0
10 + 1 = 11	11 - 10 = 1
7 + 4 = 7+3+1=11	11 - 7 = 11-1-6 = 4
8 + 3 = 8+2+1=11	11 - 8 = 11-1-7 = 3
9 + 2 = 9+1+1=11	11 - 9 = 11-1-8 = 2
6 + 5 = 6+4+1=11	11 - 7 = 11-1-6 = 4
8 + 3 = 8+2+1=11	11 - 4 = 11-1-3 = 7

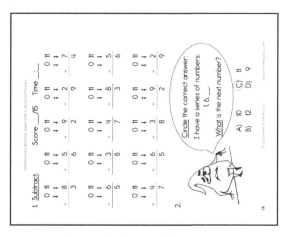

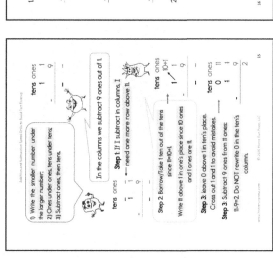

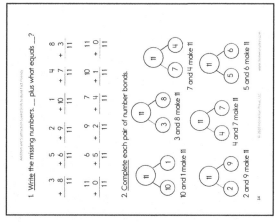

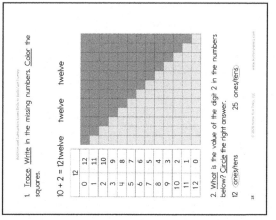

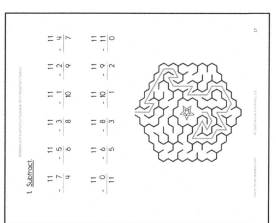

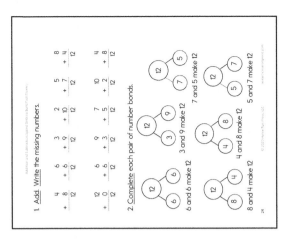
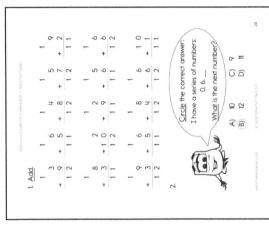
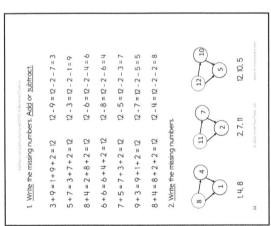
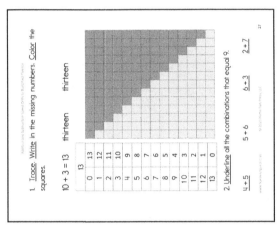
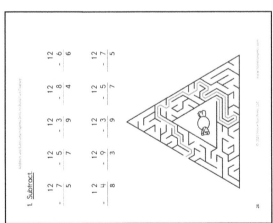
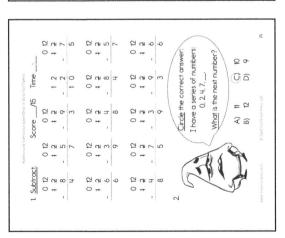

Page 29

1. Write the missing numbers. Add or subtract:

11 + 2 = 13	13 - 2 = 11
0 + 13 = 13	13 - 0 = 13

9 + 4 = 9+1+3=13   13 - 9 = 13-3-6=4
8 + 5 = 8+2+3=13   13 - 8 = 13-3-5=5
7 + 6 = 7+3+3=13   13 - 7 = 13-3-4=6
5 + 7 = 3+7+2=12   13 - 5 = 13-3-2=8
4 + 9 = 1+9+3=13   13 - 4 = 13-3-1=9

Page 30

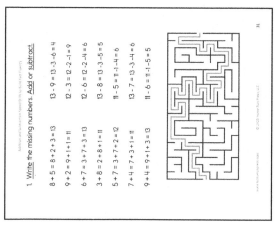

1. Write the missing numbers. Add or subtract:

3 + 10 = 13   13 - 3 = 10
1 + 11 = 12   13 - 1 = 12

7 + 6 = 7+3+3=13   13 - 7 = 13-3-4=6
9 + 4 = 9+1+3=13   13 - 6 = 13-3-3=7
8 + 5 = 8+2+3=13   13 - 9 = 13-3-6=4
4 + 9 = 1+9+3=13   13 - 8 = 13-3-5=5
6 + 7 = 3+7+3=13   13 - 4 = 13-3-1=9

Page 31

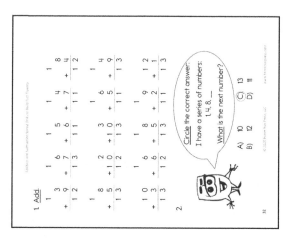

1. Write the missing numbers. Add or subtract:

8 + 5 = 8+2+3=13   13 - 9 = 13-3-6=4
9 + 2 = 9+1+1=11   12 - 3 = 12-2-1=9
6 + 7 = 3+7+3=13   12 - 6 = 12-2-4=6
3 + 8 = 2+8+1=11   13 - 8 = 13-3-5=5
5 + 7 = 3+7+2=12   11 - 5 = 11-1-4=6
7 + 4 = 7+3+1=11   13 - 7 = 13-3-4=6
9 + 4 = 9+1+3=13   11 - 6 = 11-1-5=5

Page 32

1. Add.

2.

Circle the correct answer:
I have a series of numbers:
1, 4, 8, ___
What is the next number?

A) 10   C) 13
B) 12   D) 11

Page 33

1. Add.

2. Complete each pair of number bonds.

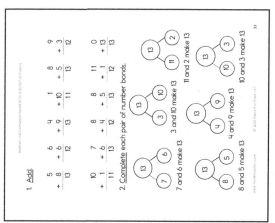

7 and 6 make 13   3 and 10 make 13   11 and 2 make 13
8 and 5 make 13   4 and 9 make 13   10 and 3 make 13

Page 34

1. Subtract.   Score ___/15   Time ___:___

2.

Circle the correct answer:
I have a series of numbers:
2, 3, 5, 8, ___
What is the next number?

A) 10   C) 11
B) 12   D) 9

Page 35

1. Subtract.

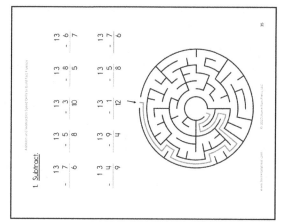

Page 36

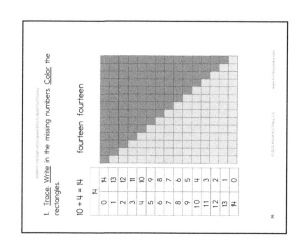

1. Trace   Write in the missing numbers. Color the rectangles.

$$10 + 4 = 14$$

fourteen   fourteen

(Page 37)

1. Write the missing numbers. Add or subtract.

| 10 + 4 = 14 | 14 - 10 = 4 |
| 13 + 1 = 14 | 14 - 13 = 1 |

5 + 9 = 1+9+4 = 14   14 - 4 - 1 = 9
6 + 8 = 2+8+4 = 14   14 - 6 = 14-4-2 = 8
7 + 7 = 3+7+4 = 14   14 - 7 = 14-4-3 = 7
8 + 6 = 8+2+4 = 14   14 - 8 = 14-4-4 = 6
9 + 5 = 9+1+4 = 14   14 - 9 = 14-4-5 = 5

(Page 38)

1. Write the missing numbers. Add or subtract.

| 12 + 2 = 14 | 14 - 12 = 2 |
| 11 + 3 = 14 | 14 - 11 = 3 |

9 + 5 = 9+1+4 = 14   14 - 7 = 14-4-3 = 7
8 + 6 = 8+2+4 = 14   14 - 9 = 14-4-5 = 5
7 + 7 = 7+3+4 = 14   14 - 5 = 14-4-1 = 9
6 + 8 = 2+8+4 = 14   14 - 6 = 14-4-2 = 8
                       14 - 7 = 14-4-3 = 7

(Page 39)

1. Write the missing numbers. Add or subtract.

| 4 + 10 = 14 | 14 - 4 = 10 |
| 3 + 11 = 14 | 14 - 3 = 11 |

7 + 6 = 7+3+3 = 13   14 - 7 = 14-4-3 = 7
8 + 6 = 8+2+4 = 14   14 - 6 = 14-4-2 = 8
9 + 5 = 9+1+4 = 14   14 - 9 = 14-4-5 = 5
7 + 7 = 3+7+4 = 14   14 - 4 = 14-4-4 = 6
5 + 9 = 1+9+4 = 14   14 - 5 = 14-4-1 = 9

(Page 40)

1. Write the missing numbers. Add or subtract.

6 + 6 = 6+4+2 = 12	14 - 9 = 14-4-5 = 5
9 + 5 = 9+1+4 = 14	12 - 5 = 12-2-3 = 7
4 + 7 = 3+7+1 = 11	11 - 6 = 11-5-5 = 5
7 + 7 = 7+3+4 = 14	14 - 8 = 14-4-4 = 6
6 + 5 = 6+4+1 = 11	13 - 5 = 13-3-2 = 8
8 + 6 = 8+2+4 = 14	14 - 7 = 14-4-3 = 7
4 + 9 = 1+9+3 = 13	12 - 6 = 12-2-4 = 6

2. Write the missing numbers.

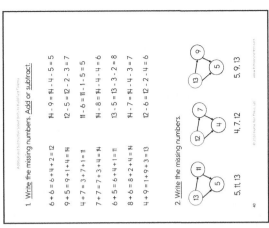

5, 11, 13   4, 7, 12   5, 9, 13

(Page 41)

1. Add.

2.

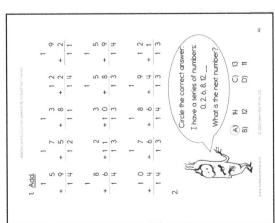

I have a series of numbers:
0, 2, 6, 8, 12, ___
What is the next number?

A) 14   C) 13
B) 12   D) 11

(Page 42)

1. Write the missing numbers. ___ plus what equals ___?

2. Complete each pair of number bonds.

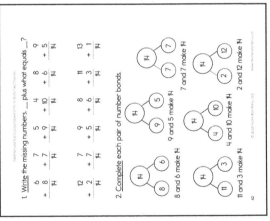

8 and 6 make 14   9 and 5 make 14
11 and 3 make 14   4 and 10 make 14
7 and 7 make 14   2 and 12 make 14

(Page 43)

1. Subtract.   Score ___/15   Time ___:___

2.

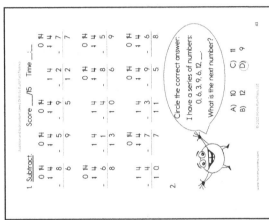

Circle the correct answer:
I have a series of numbers:
0, 6, 3, 9, 6, 12, ___
What is the next number?

A) 10   C) 11
B) 12   D) 9

(Page 44)

1. Subtract.

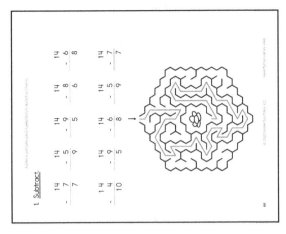

96

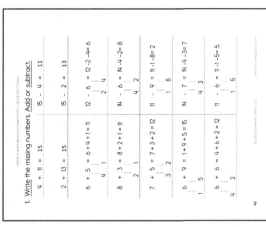

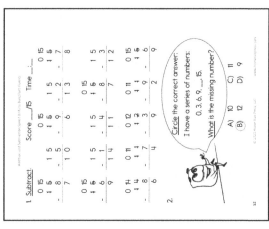

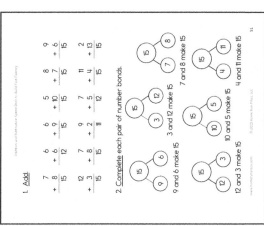

1. Write the missing numbers. Add or subtract.

10 + 5 = 15	15 − 10 = 5
14 + 1 = 15	15 − 14 = 1

6 + 9 = 1 + 9 + 5 = 15   15 − 6 = 15 − 5 − 1 = 9

7 + 8 = 2 + 8 + 5 = 15   15 − 7 = 15 − 5 − 2 = 8

8 + 7 = 8 + 2 + 5 = 15   15 − 8 = 15 − 5 − 3 = 7

9 + 6 = 9 + 1 + 4 = 14   15 − 9 = 15 − 5 − 4 = 6

9 + 6 = 9 + 1 + 5 = 15   15 − 8 = 15 − 5 − 3 = 7

1. Write the missing numbers. Add or subtract.

12 + 3 = 15	15 − 12 = 3
13 + 2 = 15	15 − 13 = 2

9 + 6 = 9 + 1 + 5 = 15   15 − 6 = 15 − 5 − 1 = 9

8 + 7 = 8 + 2 + 5 = 15   15 − 7 = 15 − 5 − 2 = 8

7 + 7 = 7 + 3 + 4 = 14   14 − 7 = 14 − 4 − 3 = 7

8 + 7 = 3 + 7 + 5 = 15   15 − 8 = 15 − 5 − 3 = 7

6 + 9 = 1 + 9 + 5 = 15   15 − 5 − 4 = 6

1. Write the missing numbers. Add or subtract.

4 + 11 = 15	15 − 4 = 11
2 + 13 = 15	15 − 2 = 13

6 + 5 = 6 + 4 + 1 = 11   12 − 6 = 12 − 2 − 4 = 6

8 + 3 = 8 + 2 + 1 = 11   14 − 6 = 14 − 4 − 2 = 8

7 + 5 = 7 + 3 + 2 = 12   11 − 9 = 11 − 1 − 8 = 2

6 + 9 = 1 + 9 + 5 = 15   14 − 7 = 14 − 3 − 3 = 7

6 + 6 = 4 + 6 + 2 = 12   11 − 6 = 11 − 1 − 5 = 5

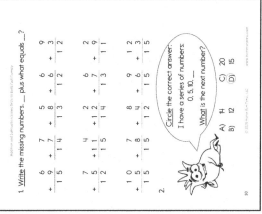

1. Write the missing numbers. __ plus what equals __?

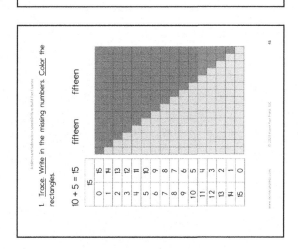

1. Trace. Write in the missing numbers. Color the rectangles.

10 + 5 = 15

fifteen   fifteen

1. Write the missing numbers. Add or subtract.

8 + 7 = 8 + 2 + 5 = 15   15 − 9 = 15 − 5 − 4 = 6

9 + 2 = 9 + 1 + 1 = 11   14 − 5 = 14 − 4 − 1 = 9

3 + 8 = 2 + 8 + 1 = 11   12 − 6 = 12 − 2 − 4 = 6

6 + 7 = 3 + 7 + 3 = 13   13 − 8 = 13 − 3 − 5 = 5

9 + 6 = 9 + 1 + 5 = 15   11 − 5 = 11 − 1 − 4 = 9

5 + 6 = 4 + 6 + 1 = 11   12 − 7 = 12 − 2 − 5 = 5

4 + 8 = 2 + 8 + 2 = 12   14 − 6 = 14 − 4 − 2 = 8

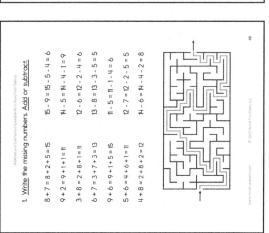

Page 53

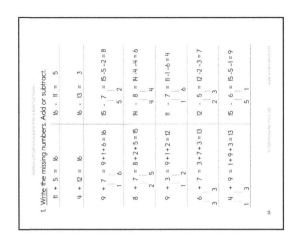

1. Subtract.

15 - 7	11 - 5	12 - 3	14 - 8	15 - 6
8	6	9	6	9

15 - 4	15 - 3	11 - 7	15 - 7
11	12	4	8

Page 54

1. Trace. Write in the missing numbers. Color the rectangles.

10 + 6 = 16

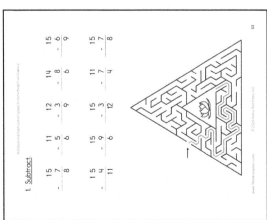

sixteen   sixteen

Page 55

1. Write the missing numbers. Add or subtract.

10 + 6 = 16	16 - 10 = 6
15 + 1 = 16	16 - 15 = 1
7 + 9 = 1+9+6 = 16	16 - 7 = 16-6-1 = 9
8 + 8 = 2+8+6 = 16	16 - 8 = 16-6-2 = 8
4 + 7 = 3+7+1 = 11	12 - 9 = 12-2-7 = 3
5 + 8 = 2+8+3 = 13	15 - 7 = 15-5-2 = 8
8 + 3 = 8+2+1 = 11	12 - 8 = 12-2-6 = 4

Page 56

1. Write the missing numbers. Add or subtract.

11 + 5 = 16	16 - 11 = 5
4 + 12 = 16	16 - 13 = 3
9 + 7 = 9+1+6 = 16	15 - 7 = 15-5-2 = 8
8 + 7 = 8+2+5 = 15	14 - 8 = 14-4-4 = 6
9 + 3 = 9+1+2 = 12	11 - 7 = 11-1-6 = 4
6 + 7 = 3+7+3 = 13	12 - 5 = 12-2-3 = 7
4 + 9 = 1+9+3 = 13	15 - 6 = 15-5-1 = 9

Page 57

1. Write the missing numbers. Add or subtract.

3 + 13 = 16	16 - 3 = 13
1 + 15 = 16	16 - 2 = 14
9 + 6 = 9+1+5 = 15	16 - 7 = 16-6-1 = 9
7 + 4 = 7+3+1 = 11	12 - 6 = 12-2-4 = 6
9 + 5 = 9+1+4 = 14	14 - 9 = 14-4-5 = 5
6 + 7 = 3+7+3 = 13	12 - 8 = 12-2-2 = 4
5 + 8 = 2+8+3 = 13	11 - 4 = 11-1-3 = 7

Page 58

1. Write the missing numbers. Add or subtract.

8 + 4 = 8+2+2 = 12	12 - 9 = 12-2-7 = 3
9 + 7 = 9+1+6 = 16	11 - 5 = 11-1-4 = 6
5 + 8 = 2+8+3 = 13	14 - 6 = 14-4-2 = 8
6 + 9 = 1+9+5 = 15	16 - 8 = 16-6-2 = 8
9 + 3 = 9+1+2 = 12	13 - 5 = 13-3-2 = 8
5 + 7 = 3+7+2 = 12	16 - 7 = 16-6-1 = 9
8 + 8 = 8+2+6 = 16	12 - 6 = 12-2-4 = 6

2. Write the missing numbers.

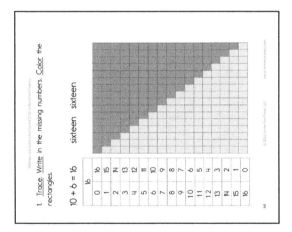

10, 8, 14, 3   6, 15, 9, 13   12, 16, 14, 7

Page 59

1. Add.

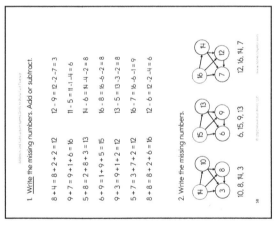

2.

Circle the correct answer.
I have a series of numbers:
0, 4, 8, 12, ___
What is the next number?

A) 20   C) 13
B) 14   D) 16

Page 60

1. Add.

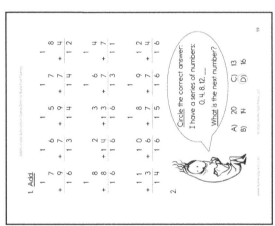

2. Complete each pair of number bonds.

10 and 6 make 16   3 and 13 make 16   7 and 9 make 16

4 and 12 make 16   5 and 11 make 16   8 and 8 make 13

1. Subtract. Score ___/15 Time ___:___

0 16 − 8 = 8	0 16 − 6 = 11	0 16 − 9 = 7	0 16 + 6 = 9
0 14 + 4 = 4	16 − 11 = 5	16 − 4 = 12	16 + 5 = 11
0 12 + 4 = 8	0 11 − 3 = 8	0 15 + 9 = 6	0 13 + 3 = 7

2. *Circle the correct answer:*
I have a series of numbers:
2, 4, 7, 11, ___
What is the next number?
A) 14   C) 15
B) 12   D) 16

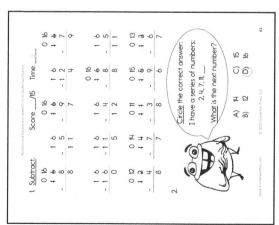

1. Subtract.

16 − 7 = 9	16 − 5 = 11	16 − 3 = 13	16 − 8 = 8	16 − 6 = 10
16 − 14 = 2	16 − 9 = 7	16 − 1 = 15	16 − 15 = 1	16 − 6 = 9

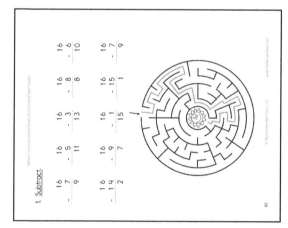

1. Trace. Write in the missing numbers. Color the rectangles.

10 + 7 = 17   seventeen   seventeen

17	
0	17
1	16
2	15
3	14
4	13
5	12
6	11
7	10
8	9
9	8
10	7
11	6
12	5
13	4
14	3
15	2
16	1
17	0

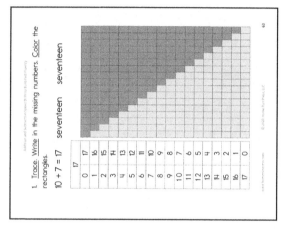

1. Write in the missing numbers. Add or subtract.

10 + 7 = 17	17 − 10 = 7
16 + 1 = 17	17 − 16 = 1
8 + 9 = 1+9+7 = 17	17 − 8 = 17−7−1 = 9
3 + 9 = 1+9+2 = 12	16 − 7 = 16−6−1 = 9
7 + 7 = 3+7+4 = 14	12 − 6 = 12−2−4 = 6
5 + 8 = 2+8+3 = 13	12 − 9 = 12−2−7 = 3
9 + 4 = 9+1+3 = 13	11 − 8 = 11−1−7 = 3

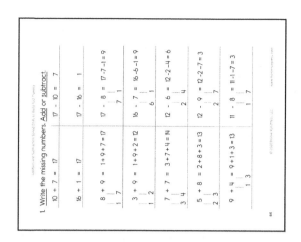

1. Write the missing numbers. Add or subtract.

12 + 5 = 17	17 − 12 = 5
4 + 13 = 17	17 − 4 = 13
9 + 8 = 1+9+7 = 17	14 − 6 = 14−4−2 = 8
8 + 5 = 8+2+3 = 13	11 − 6 = 11−1−5 = 5
9 + 7 = 9+1+6 = 16	15 − 8 = 15−5−3 = 7
6 + 7 = 3+7+3 = 13	11 − 5 = 11−1−4 = 6
6 + 9 = 1+9+5 = 15	17 − 9 = 17−7−2 = 8

1. Write the missing numbers. Add or subtract.

8 + 8 = 8+2+6 = 16	15 − 9 = 15−5−4 = 6
9 + 8 = 9+1+7 = 17	14 − 5 = 14−4−1 = 9
5 + 6 = 4+6+1 = 11	13 − 6 = 13−3−3 = 7
6 + 7 = 3+7+3 = 13	17 − 8 = 17−7−1 = 9
9 + 4 = 9+1+3 = 13	11 − 5 = 11−1−4 = 6
7 + 7 = 3+7+4 = 14	13 − 9 = 13−3−6 = 4
6 + 8 = 2+8+4 = 14	12 − 6 = 12−2−4 = 6

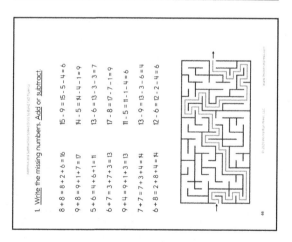

1. Add.

2. *Circle the correct answer:*
I have a series of numbers:
0, 3, 8, ___
What is the next number?
A) 14   C) 15
B) 17   D) 13

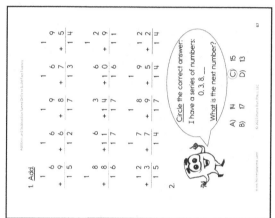

1. Add.

2. **Complete each pair of number bonds.**

11 and 6 make 17
3 and 14 make 17
7 and 10 make 17
8 and 9 make 17
4 and 13 make 17
5 and 12 make 17

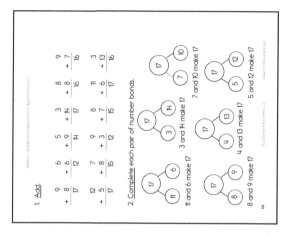

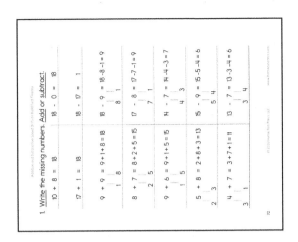

1. Trace. Write in the missing numbers. Color the rectangles.

eighteen eighteen

10 + 8 = 18

18	
0	18
1	17
2	16
3	15
4	14
5	13
6	12
7	11
8	10
9	9
10	8
11	7
12	6
13	5
14	4
15	3
16	2
17	1
18	0

71

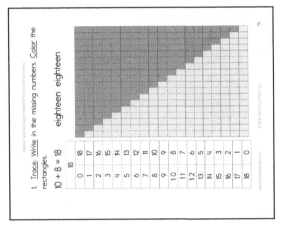

1. Write the missing numbers. Add or subtract:

10 + 8 = 18   18 - 0 = 18
17 + 1 = 18   18 - 17 = 1
9 + 9 = 9+1+8 = 18   18 - 9 = 18-8-1 = 9
8 + 7 = 8+2+5=15   17 - 8 = 17-7-1 = 9
9 + 6 = 9+1+5=15   14 - 7 = 14-4-3 = 7
5 + 8 = 2+8+3=13   15 - 9 = 15-5-4 = 6
4 + 7 = 3+7+1=11   13 - 7 = 13-3-4 = 6

72

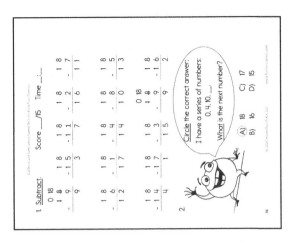

1. Subtract: Score ___/15   Time __:__

Circle the correct answer:
I have a series of numbers:
0, 4, 10, ___
What is the next number?
A) 18   C) 17
B) 16   D) 15

76

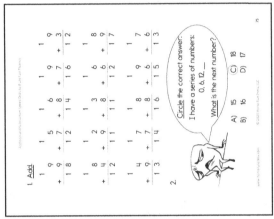

1. Add.

Circle the correct answer:
I have a series of numbers:
0, 6, 12, ___
What is the next number?
A) 15   C) 18
B) 16   D) 17

75

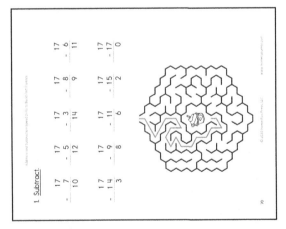

1. Subtract:

70

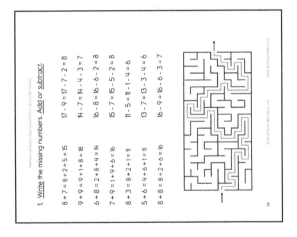

1. Write the missing numbers. Add or subtract:

8 + 7 = 8+2+5=15   17 - 9 = 17-7-2 = 8
9 + 9 = 9+1+8 = 18   14 - 7 = 14-4-3 = 7
6 + 8 = 2+8+4=14   16 - 8 = 16-6-2 = 8
7 + 9 = 1+9+6=16   15 - 7 = 15-5-2 = 8
8 + 3 = 8+2+1=11   11 - 5 = 11-1-4 = 6
5 + 6 = 4+6+1=11   13 - 7 = 13-3-4 = 6
8 + 8 = 8+2+6=16   16 - 9 = 16-6-3 = 7

74

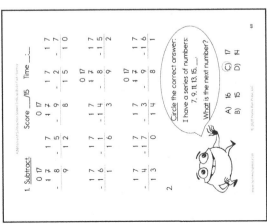

1. Subtract: Score ___/15   Time __:__

Circle the correct answer:
I have a series of numbers:
7, 9, 11, 13, 15, ___
What is the next number?
A) 16   C) 17
B) 15   D) 14

69

1. Write the missing numbers. Add or subtract:

13 + 5 = 18   18 - 7 = 11
12 + 6 = 18   18 - 14 = 4
8 + 6 = 8+2+4=14   16 - 8 = 16-6-2 = 8
9 + 7 = 9+1+6=16   14 - 8 = 14-4-6 = 6
6 + 5 = 6+4+1=11   11 - 9 = 11-1-8 = 2
8 + 9 = 9+1+7=17   13 - 4 = 13-3-1 = 9
9 + 9 = 1+9+8=18   17 - 8 = 17-7-1 = 9

73

100

Page 77

1. Trace. Write in the missing numbers. Color the rectangles.

$10 + 9 = 19$ nineteen nineteen

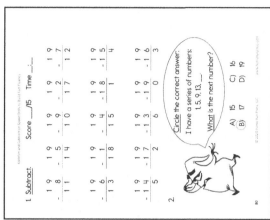

Page 78

1. Write the missing numbers. Add or subtract:

$8 + 8 = 8 + 2 + 6 = 16$	$18 - 9 = 18 - 8 - 1 = 9$
$9 + 9 = 9 + 1 + 8 = 18$	$13 - 5 = 13 - 3 - 2 = 8$
$5 + 6 = 5 + 4 + 6 + 1 = 11$	$14 - 8 = 14 - 4 - 4 = 6$
$6 + 7 = 3 + 7 + 3 = 13$	$16 - 9 = 16 - 6 - 3 = 7$
$9 + 4 = 9 + 1 + 3 = 13$	$13 - 7 = 13 - 3 - 4 = 6$
$7 + 7 = 7 + 3 + 4 = 14$	$16 - 9 = 16 - 6 - 3 = 7$
$8 + 3 = 8 + 2 + 1 = 11$	$12 - 7 = 12 - 2 - 5 = 5$

2. Draw the missing arrows. The arrow means: ___ is greater than ___:

6, 9, 15, 19   2, 4, 13, 16   7, 10, 14, 18

Page 79

1. Add. Write the missing numbers.

(vertical addition problems, each summing to 19)

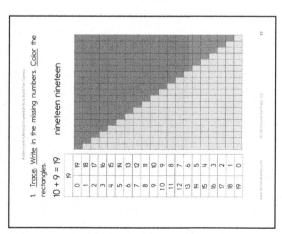

Circle the correct answer.
I have a series of numbers: 3, 4, 7, 12, ___
What is the next number?

A) 18   C) 15
B) 19   D) 17

Page 80

1. Subtract.   Score ___/15   Time __:__

(vertical subtraction problems with 19)

Circle the correct answer.
I have a series of numbers: 1, 5, 9, 13, ___
What is the next number?

A) 15   C) 16
B) 17   D) 19

Page 81

1. Trace. Write in the missing numbers. Color the rectangles.

$10 + 10 = 20$ twenty twenty

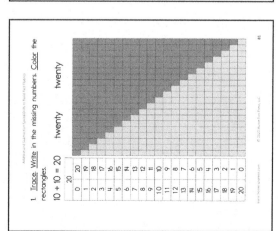

Page 82

1. Write the missing numbers. Add or subtract:

$14 + 6 = 10+4+6=20$	$20 - 14 = 10+10-4 = 6$
$15 + 5 = 10+5+5=20$	$20 - 5 = 10+10-5 = 15$
$11 + 9 = 10+1+9=20$	$20 - 16 = 10+10-6=4$
$18 + 2 = 10+8+2=20$	$20 - 11 = 10+10-1=9$
$3 + 17 = 10+3+7=20$	$20 - 8 = 10+10-8 = 12$
$12 + 8 = 10+2+8=20$	$20 - 13 = 10+10-3=7$
$19 + 1 = 10+9+1=20$	$20 - 4 = 10+10-4 = 16$

Page 83

1. Write the missing numbers. Add or subtract:

$13 + 7 = 10+3+7=20$	$20 - 15 = 10+10-5-5$ 5
$5 + 15 = 10+5+5=20$	$20 - 2 = 10+10-2 = 18$
$17 + 3 = 10+7+3=20$	$20 - 19 = 10+10-9=1$
$16 + 4 = 10+6+4=20$	$20 - 4 = 10+10-4 = 16$
$1 + 19 = 10+1+9=20$	$20 - 8 = 10+10-8 = 12$
$7 + 13 = 10+7+3=20$	$20 - 17 = 10+10-7=3$
$8 + 12 = 10+8+2=20$	$20 - 9 = 10+10-9 = 11$

Page 84

1. Write the missing numbers. Add or subtract:

$9 + 11 = 10+9+1=20$	$20 - 12 = 10+10-2=8$
$6 + 14 = 10+6+4=20$	$20 - 7 = 10+10-7 = 13$
$18 + 2 = 10+8+2=20$	$20 - 1 = 10+10-1 = 19$
$16 + 4 = 10+6+4=20$	$20 - 18 = 10+10-8=2$
$5 + 15 = 10+5+5=20$	$20 - 6 = 10+10-6 = 14$
$7 + 13 = 10+7+3=20$	$20 - 3 = 10+10-3 = 17$
$9 + 11 = 10+9+1=20$	$20 - 7 = 10+10-7 = 13$

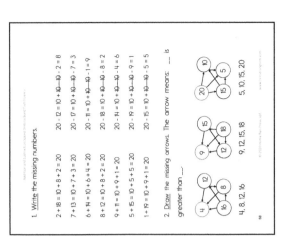

1. Write the missing numbers.

14 + 6 = 10 + 4 + 6 = 20
19 + 1 = 10 + 9 + 1 = 20
15 + 5 = 10 + 5 + 5 = 20
16 + 4 = 10 + 6 + 4 = 20
17 + 3 = 10 + 7 + 3 = 20
12 + 8 = 10 + 2 + 8 = 20
13 + 7 = 10 + 3 + 7 = 20

20 - 9 = 10 + 10 - 9 = 11
20 - 5 = 10 + 10 - 5 = 15
20 - 6 = 10 + 10 - 6 = 14
20 - 8 = 10 + 10 - 8 = 12
20 - 1 = 10 + 10 - 1 = 19
20 - 7 = 10 + 10 - 7 = 13
20 - 3 = 10 + 10 - 3 = 17

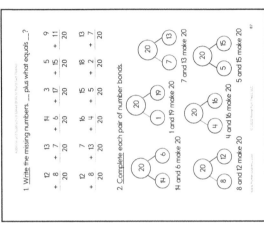

1. Write the missing numbers. __ plus what equals __?

1 1	1 6	1 5	1 2	1 9
+ 9	+ 4	+ 5	+ 8	+ 1
2 0	2 0	2 0	2 0	2 0
8	9	3	6	1
+ 1 2	+ 1 1	+ 1 7	+ 1 4	+ 1 9
2 0	2 0	2 0	2 0	2 0
1 7	4	1 8	1 9	1 2
+ 3	+ 1 6	+ 2	+ 1	+ 8
2 0	2 0	2 0	2 0	2 0

2.

Circle the correct answer:
I have a series of numbers:
5, 10, 15, __
What is the next number?

A) 16
B) 22
C) 20
D) 25

1. Write the missing numbers. __ plus what equals __?

12	13	14	3	5	9
+ 8	+ 7	+ 6	+ 17	+ 15	+ 11
20	20	20	20	20	20
12	7	16	15	18	13
+ 8	+ 13	+ 4	+ 5	+ 2	+ 7
20	20	20	20	20	20

2. Complete each pair of number bonds.

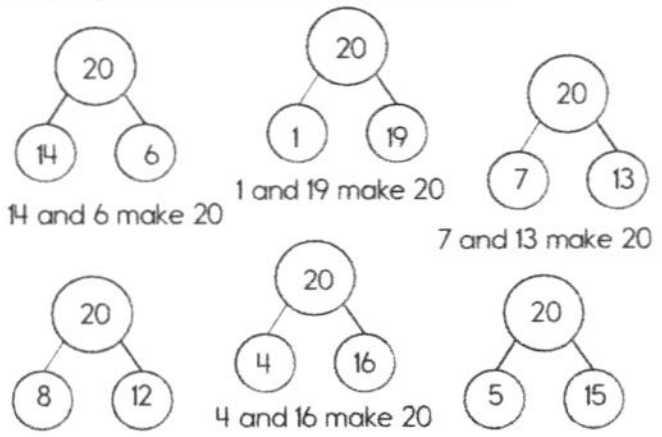

14 and 6 make 20
1 and 19 make 20
7 and 13 make 20
8 and 12 make 20
4 and 16 make 20
5 and 15 make 20

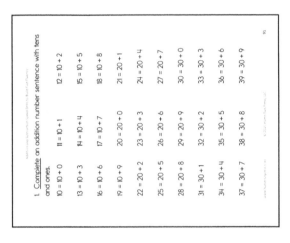

1. Write the missing numbers.

2 + 18 = 10 + 8 + 2 = 20
7 + 13 = 10 + 7 + 3 = 20
6 + 14 = 10 + 6 + 4 = 20
8 + 12 = 10 + 8 + 2 = 20
9 + 11 = 10 + 9 + 1 = 20
5 + 15 = 10 + 5 + 5 = 20
1 + 19 = 10 + 9 + 1 = 20

20 - 12 = 10 + ~~10~~ ~~10~~ - 2 = 8
20 - 17 = 10 + ~~10~~ ~~10~~ - 7 = 3
20 - 11 = 10 + ~~10~~ ~~10~~ - 1 = 9
20 - 18 = 10 + ~~10~~ ~~10~~ - 8 = 2
20 - 14 = 10 + ~~10~~ ~~10~~ - 4 = 6
20 - 19 = 10 + ~~10~~ ~~10~~ - 9 = 1
20 - 15 = 10 + ~~10~~ ~~10~~ - 5 = 5

2. Draw the missing arrows. The arrow means: __ is greater than __.

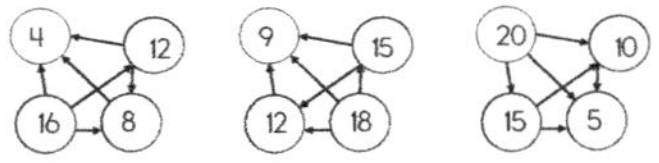

4, 8, 12, 16 9, 12, 15, 18 5, 10, 15, 20

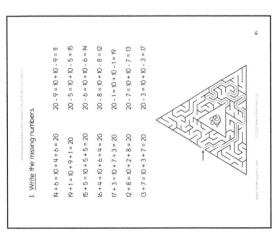

1. Subtract. Score ___/15 Time __:__

1 10	1 10	1 10	1 10	1 10
~~2~~ ~~0~~	~~2~~ ~~0~~	~~2~~ ~~0~~	~~2~~ ~~0~~	~~2~~ ~~0~~
- 1 8	- 1 5	- 1 9	- 1 2	- 1 7
2	5	1	8	3
1 10	1 10	1 10	1 10	1 10
~~2~~ ~~0~~	~~2~~ ~~0~~	~~2~~ ~~0~~	~~2~~ ~~0~~	~~2~~ ~~0~~
- 1 6	- 1 1	- 1 4	- 1 8	- 1 5
4	9	6	2	5
1 10	1 10	1 10	1 10	1 10
~~2~~ ~~0~~	~~2~~ ~~0~~	~~2~~ ~~0~~	~~2~~ ~~0~~	~~2~~ ~~0~~
- 1 5	- 1 7	- 1 3	- 1 9	- 1 6
5	3	7	1	4

2.

Circle the correct answer:
I have a series of numbers:
1, 5, 11, __.
What is the next number?

A) 15
B) 16
C) 19
D) 20

1. Subtract.

20	20	20	20	20
- 7	- 5	- 3	- 8	- 6
13	15	17	12	14
20	20	20	20	20
- 4	- 9	- 1	- 5	- 7
16	11	19	15	13

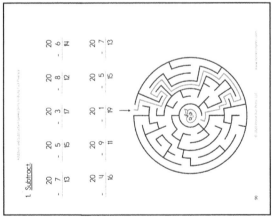

1. Complete an addition number sentence with tens and ones.

10 = 10 + 0	11 = 10 + 1	12 = 10 + 2
13 = 10 + 3	14 = 10 + 4	15 = 10 + 5
16 = 10 + 6	17 = 10 + 7	18 = 10 + 8
19 = 10 + 9	20 = 20 + 0	21 = 20 + 1
22 = 20 + 2	23 = 20 + 3	24 = 20 + 4
25 = 20 + 5	26 = 20 + 6	27 = 20 + 7
28 = 20 + 8	29 = 20 + 9	30 = 30 + 0
31 = 30 + 1	32 = 30 + 2	33 = 30 + 3
34 = 30 + 4	35 = 30 + 5	36 = 30 + 6
37 = 30 + 7	38 = 30 + 8	39 = 30 + 9

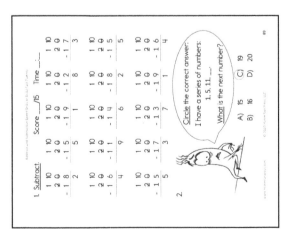

Made in the USA
Coppell, TX
21 July 2022

80258457R00057